Summary of Contents

Preface xxi

1. The Changing Face of Marketing 1

2. 21st Century Public Relations and Media 7

3. Turn Page Views into Profit 33

4. Search Engine Optimization 49

5. Social Media 77

6. Email Marketing 95

7. Affiliate Marketing 113

8. Online Advertising 129

9. Tying It All Together 161

Index 175

ONLINE MARKETING INSIDE OUT

BY **BRANDON ELEY**
& SHAYNE TILLEY

Online Marketing Inside Out

by Brandon Eley and Shayne Tilley

Copyright © 2009 SitePoint Pty. Ltd.

Expert Reviewer: Ted Sindzinski **Managing Editor:** Chris Wyness

Expert Reviewer: Jeanne S. Jennings **Technical Director:** Kevin Yank

Expert Reviewer: Patrick O'Keefe **Indexer:** Russell Brooks

Technical Editor: Raena Jackson Armitage **Cover Design:** Alex Walker

Editor: Kelly Steele

Printing History:

   First Edition: May 2009

Published by SitePoint Pty. Ltd.

48 Cambridge Street
Collingwood, Victoria, Australia 3066
Web: www.sitepoint.com
Email: business@sitepoint.com

ISBN 978-0-9805768-2-5
Printed and bound in Canada

About the Authors

In 1999, Brandon Eley started 2BigFeet.com (http://2bigfeet.com) in the then untapped market for large-sized shoes. The need for an ecommerce web site led to his trial-by-fire indoctrination into web development and online marketing. In addition to owning 2BigFeet, Brandon is also the Interactive Director for Kelsey Advertising & Design, where he oversees interactive projects and online marketing campaigns, and blogs at http://brandoneley.com.

Shayne Tilley has had a healthy addiction for the Web since building his very first web site back in 1997. With extensive experience in both traditional and online forms of direct marketing, Shayne has traveled the path all marketers must walk to modernize their marketing mix. Now as the Marketing Manager for SitePoint, he continually pushes the boundaries of online marketing everyday for one of the world's largest web sites, sitepoint.com. You can follow Shayne 140 characters at a time via Twitter at http://twitter.com/ShayneT.

About the Expert Reviewers

Jeanne S. Jennings is a recognized expert and published author in the field of email marketing. She helps companies become more effective and more profitable online by focusing on all aspects of email marketing including strategy, tactics, creative, and testing. Jeanne has advised a wide variety of large and small organizations including Hasbro, Verizon, and Weight Watchers. Learn more at http://jeannejennings.com.

Patrick O'Keefe is the founder and owner of the iFroggy Network (http://ifroggy.com), an Internet network featuring numerous forums and communities. An experienced community manager since 2000, he is the author of the book *Managing Online Forums* (New York: AMACOM, 2008), a practical guide to managing online forums, communities, and social spaces. He maintains a personal blog at http://patrickokeefe.com.

Ted Sindzinski is an Internet marketing professional with experience managing acquisition and retention marketing campaigns, using search, display, and email tactics. Ted is well versed in site and conversion optimization and develops marketing solutions for business-to-consumer companies ranging from startups to Fortune 500s.

About the Technical Editor

Raena Jackson Armitage made her way to SitePoint via a circuitous route involving web development, training, and speaking. A lifelong Mac fangirl, she's written for *The Mac Observer* and *About This Particular Macintosh*. Raena likes knitting, reading, and riding her bike around Melbourne in search of the perfect all-day breakfast. Raena's personal web site is at http://raena.net.

About the Technical Director

As Technical Director for SitePoint, Kevin Yank oversees all of its technical publications—books, articles, newsletters, and blogs. He has written over 50 articles for SitePoint, but is best known for his book, *Build Your Own Database Driven Website Using PHP & MySQL*. Kevin lives in Melbourne, Australia, and enjoys performing improvised comedy theatre and flying light aircraft.

About SitePoint

SitePoint specializes in publishing fun, practical, and easy-to-understand content for web professionals. Visit http://sitepoint.com to access our books, newsletters, articles, and community forums.

*To my wife Tracy, for putting up
with a workaholic, and to Peyton
and Ellis for putting up with
Mommy's cooking when Daddy
worked late!*

—Brandon

*To my beautiful fiancée Justine,
mother Alida, father Neil, and
sister Belinda. Thank-you for
making my world a better place.*

—Shayne

Table of Contents

Preface xxi

  Who Should Read This Book? xxi

  What's Covered in This Book? xxi

    Chapter 1: The Changing Face of Marketing xxi

    Chapter 2: 21st Century Public Relations and Media xxii

    Chapter 3: Turn Page Views into Profit xxii

    Chapter 4: Search Engine Optimization xxii

    Chapter 5: Social Media xxii

    Chapter 6: Email Marketing xxii

    Chapter 7: Affiliate Marketing xxii

    Chapter 8: Online Advertising xxiii

    Chapter 9: Tying It All Together xxiii

  The SitePoint Forums xxiii

  This Book's Web Site xxiii

  The SitePoint Newsletters xxiv

  Your Feedback xxiv

  Conventions Used in This Book xxiv

    Tips, Notes, and Warnings xxiv

  Acknowledgements xxv

    Brandon Eley xxv

    Shayne Tilley xxv

Chapter 1   **The Changing Face of Marketing** 1

  Why is Online Marketing So Important? 2

  It's All About the People 2

Technical, Fast, and Complex 2

Beyond the Web Geeks 3

Starting Your Online Journey 3

    Starting a New Business 3

    Expanding an Existing Business 4

Easy as 1, 2, 3 4

    Attract 4

    Engage 4

    Transact 4

Why You'll Love Online Marketing 5

    Results Are Instantaneous 5

    New Levels of Customer Interaction 5

    A Team Player 5

    Instant Global Market 5

    Opportunities Are Everywhere 6

Start Me Up! 6

Chapter 2   21st Century Public Relations and Media

Chapter 2   **21st Century Public Relations and Media** 7

What is Public Relations? 8

Press Releases 8

    Press Releases in the 21st Century 9

    When to Write a Press Release 9

    Anatomy of a Press Release 10

    Stand Out from the Crowd 14

    Distribute Press Releases 15

Use Blogs to Spread the Word 17

    Find Influential Blogs and Web Sites 18

    Comment on Influential Blogs 19

Send Your Press Releases Directly to Influential Bloggers 20

Smaller Blogs Copy Bigger Blogs 21

Non-traditional Marketing 21

Non-traditional Marketing Offline 21

Non-traditional Marketing Online 23

Words of Wisdom 25

Selling the Owner on Online Marketing 26

Modern Monitoring of Press Coverage 27

What Should You Track? 28

Social Media Monitoring Services 29

Someone Wrote about Me! What Now? 30

Summary 31

Chapter 3   **Turn Page Views into Profit** 33

Usability 34

Improving Usability: Test Early, Test Often 34

Conducting a Test 35

Interpreting and Acting 37

Employing Usability Experts 37

Accessibility 37

Why care about accessibility? 38

How to Check Your Web Site's Accessibility 39

Performance and Scalability 40

Scalability 41

Battle of the Browsers 41

Screen Resolutions and Monitor Sizes 42

Varying Browsers and Versions 42

Test Your Site 42

Your Homepage 43

Clearly Explain Who You Are 43

Include a Search 43

Provide Fresh Web Site Content 43

Keep Your Corporate Information Together 44

Design that Enhances 44

Lovely Landing Pages 44

Focus on One Objective 44

Use Visuals to Drive Focus 45

Above the Fold 45

Page Layout 46

What's your value proposition? 46

Building Customer Confidence 46

Testing Conversions 46

A/B testing 47

Multivariate Testing 47

An Evolving Entity 48

Chapter 4   **Search Engine Optimization** 49

Understanding Search Engines 50

The Role of a Search Engine 50

Search Engine Results Pages 50

How Search Engines Collect Information 51

How a Search Engine Determines Rank 51

The Big Three 53

The Different Hats of SEO 53

Creating Your Own SEO Strategy 54

Keywords 54

Identify Generic Keywords 55

Add More Focused Terms 56

Phrases and Modifiers 56

Singular and Plural 56

Use Variations and Misspellings 56

Watch Out for Common Words 57

Identifying Your Ideal Keywords 57

Localization 58

Using Brand Names 58

Deciding Which Terms to Target 58

Relevance 60

Return on Investment 62

Site Design 63

Page Design Elements 63

Heading Elements 63

Paragraphs 64

Page Title 64

Hyperlinks 64

Meta Elements 65

Web Site Design Issues and SEO 65

Content 66

Integrating Keywords into Your Content 66

Duplicate Copy 68

Tips for Spider-friendly Sites 68

Popularity 69

Build Incoming Links 70

Great Content Means Great Links 71

Opportunity Knocks 72

Welcome, Spiders! 72

Measuring and Tracking Success 73

More on SEO 74

Engaging the Services of an SEO Expert 74

The Future of SEO 74

The Start of a Beautiful Friendship 75

Chapter 5   **Social Media** 77

What is Social Networking? 78

    What is Social Media? 78

Social Content Goes Mainstream 78

The End of Interruption Marketing 79

Word of Mouth: Far Reaching and Fast 80

Grab the Opportunity 80

Types of Social Media 81

    Social Networking Sites 81

    Blogging 81

    Microblogging 82

    Photo and Video Sharing 82

    Bookmarks 83

    Social News 83

    Podcasts 83

    Online Forums 84

The Social Media Mind-set 84

    Being Human 84

Starting Off with Social Media 85

    Step 1: Listen 86

    Step 2: Join 87

    Step 3: Participate 88

    Step 4: Create 89

Problems and Pitfalls 91

    Privacy 91

    Transparency's Double-edged Sword 92

Establish a Clear Social Media Policy 92

Trademarks and Copyright 93

Let's Start Socializing! 93

Chapter 6   Email Marketing 95

Email's Undeserved Bad Rap 95

Different Types of Email Communication 97

Educational Communication 97

News and Updates 97

Direct Sales Messages 98

Housekeeping 98

Permission 98

Building Your Email List 99

News and Updates 99

Ask Your Customers 99

Giveaways 99

Perks 100

A Positive Call to Action 100

Offline Lead Generation 100

The Technical Side of Email 101

Managing Your Email Lists 101

Designing Your Emails 102

Sender's Details 102

Message Subject 103

Message Body 104

Avoiding Spam Filters 105

Your Landing Page 106

HTML versus Plain Text 106

Before You Send 107

Let's Take a Breather 108

Planning Your Email Marketing Campaigns 108

Best Times to Send 109

Segmentation: Targeting Your Emails 109

Sequencing 110

Frequency and Scheduling 110

Measure, Test, Optimize, and Refine 111

Where to Find More Information 112

Chapter 7   Affiliate Marketing 113

What is affiliate marketing? 114

What are the benefits of affiliate marketing? 114

The Risks and Pitfalls of Affiliate Marketing 115

Types of Affiliate Web Sites 116

Ingredients for a Great Affiliate Program 117

Under the Hood 119

Choosing an Affiliate System 120

Your Commission Model 121

Bonuses and Incentives 122

Prompt Payment and Outstanding Accuracy 122

The Affiliate Agreement 123

Recruiting Affiliates 124

Working with Your Affiliates for Shared Success 125

Research Your Competitors 126

Summing Up 127

Chapter 8   Online Advertising 129

What's up with traditional advertising? 129

The Good and the Bad 130

Supplement Your Online Campaigns 131
Split Up Your Marketing Budget 131
How Online Ads Are Better 131
Measurability 131
Highly Targeted 132
Permission Marketing 132
Interaction 132
Standard Advertising Attributes 133
Types of Ads 133
Ways to Purchase 134
Targeting for Better Results 135
The Importance of Targeting 135
Keyword Targeting 135
Demographic Targeting 136
Behavioral Targeting 136
Identifying Past Visitors 136
Geotargeting 137
Determining What to Target 137
Advertising on Search Engines 138
Where to Advertise 138
Organizational Structure 139
Campaigns and Ad Groups 139
Selecting Keywords 141
Writing an Effective Ad 143
Designing Display Ads 145
Limiting Yourself with a Budget 147
Launch Your Ads 149
Reviewing Your Campaign 150
Online Advertising Metrics 150
Determining Success 151

Optimizing Based on Metrics 152

Advertising on Social Networks 153

You've Never Seen Targeting Like This 153

The Price is Right (Now) 154

Like an Old Friend 154

Tracking 155

Seize the Day! 155

Using an Agency 155

Should You Hire an Agency? 156

What to Look For When Choosing an Agency 157

Look for Personality 158

Smaller Budgets 158

Advertising on Your Own Web Site 159

The Homepage 159

Up-sell 159

Summary 160

Chapter 9   Tying It All Together 161

What have you learned so far? 161

Achieving the Best Possible Reach 161

The Wonderful World of Search 162

The New Frontier of Social Media 162

Engaging Email Marketing 162

Affiliate Marketing 162

Online Advertising 162

Pick and Choose, or All of the Above? 163

Creating Your Online Marketing Strategy 163

The Idea 163

Your Value Proposition 164

Visualizing Your Journey 164

Finding Dependencies and Synergies 164

Creating a Customer Contact Model 165

Defining Customer Life Cycle Models 165

Creating a Testing and Evaluation Plan 166

Customer Research 167

Setting Goals 167

Establishing Goals That Are Measurable and Achievable 167

Identifying Your Revenue Generators 168

Identifying Your Key Performance Indicators 168

Milestones 169

Seasonal Variation 169

The Stages of Marketing Planning 170

Writing a Detailed Campaign Plan 170

A Campaign Approach 170

A Channel Approach 172

Your Marketing Plan 172

Ready to Roll 173

Index 175

Preface

Relying on mainstream media to break stories is oh, so 1990s. Marketing is changing, and it's changing fast. As fresh avenues of communication have arisen, traditional marketing tactics of yesteryear are becoming less effective. It's time to embrace a whole new way to build your brand, find new customers, and add value.

The Web is playing a critical role in this transformation, and it's absolutely crucial that you understand how this works. We're sure you're going to love this brave new world of online marketing.

Who Should Read This Book?

If you have a web site and you want to promote it, but are unsure where to start, this book is for you.

The book covers all you need to know to start promoting your business online. It steps you through all the elements of an effective online marketing strategy: from leading edge social media techniques, right through to more traditional activities like email, affiliate programs, and advertising campaigns. We've kept this book very practical, so that you'll be able to start campaigns straight away. And we've stayed away from "here today, gone tomorrow" marketing approaches—while online marketing is an ever-changing field, the techniques we'll show you are here to stay.

What's Covered in This Book?

Many different techniques come together to form a modern marketing campaign. We've covered a number of tried and true approaches.

Chapter 1: The Changing Face of Marketing

Why is online marketing so important? Do I need to be a web geek to understand how it works? In this chapter we'll introduce some of the key ideas and principles you'll need to understand before you set out on your online marketing journey.

Chapter 2: 21st Century Public Relations and Media

The tools and techniques to promote yourself online are available to anyone. In this chapter you'll discover how easy it is to put your message in front of millions of hungry consumers without being at the mercy of mainstream media.

Chapter 3: Turn Page Views into Profit

Your web site is the foundation of your online marketing program. While your campaigning might bring millions of eyeballs to your front door, it means little if your web site fails to convert those visitors into customers—this chapter will show you how.

Chapter 4: Search Engine Optimization

For many web surfers, a search engine is the number one starting point for finding information on the Web. How well your site performs in search engines can make the difference between a handful of visitors or millions. This chapter will show you how to make the most of the search engine crowd.

Chapter 5: Social Media

Facebook, Twitter, MySpace—you've probably heard about them, and perhaps you've used them, but have you thought about how your business can benefit from them? Social networking on the Web can deliver great gains to your business. This chapter will show you the right way to establish yourself in social media spaces.

Chapter 6: Email Marketing

Email has been around for years, but effective email marketing strategies are often forgotten. There are many advantages to email marketing—we'll walk you through every step towards a successful email marketing strategy.

Chapter 7: Affiliate Marketing

Imagine an army of salesmen all over the world who are promoting your products and services, day and night. With affiliate marketing, this is more than just a daydream—for many businesses, it's a part of life. This chapter will show you how to build your own online sales force by creating an affiliate marketing program.

Chapter 8: Online Advertising

Online advertising can take many forms, and with competition growing every day, the need for efficient online advertising that stands out in a crowd is more important than ever. In this chapter you'll discover how to plan, implement, test, and optimize your online advertising campaigns.

Chapter 9: Tying It All Together

By the time you've reached this chapter, you'll have developed an awesome arsenal of online marketing weaponry. Regardless of how good your weapons are though, without a plan, you'll just end up shooting yourself in the foot. This chapter will show you how to transform marketing tactics into a powerful plan.

The SitePoint Forums

The SitePoint Forums[1] are discussion forums where you can ask questions about anything related to web design, development, hosting, and marketing. You may, of course, answer questions, too. That's how a discussion forum site works—some people ask, some people answer—and most people do a bit of both. Sharing your knowledge benefits others and strengthens the community. A lot of fun and experienced web designers and developers hang out there. It's a good way to learn new stuff, have questions answered in a hurry, and just have fun.

The Manage Your Site forum has subforums devoted to marketing tips, ecommerce, advertising, and more.[2] It's free to sign up, and it takes just a few minutes.

This Book's Web Site

No book is perfect, and we expect that watchful readers will be able to spot at least one or two mistakes before the end of this one. The Errata page on the book's web site will always have the latest information about known typographical errors and updates. You'll find the book's web site at http://www.sitepoint.com/books/marketing1/. If you find a problem, you'll also be able to report it here.

---

[1] http://www.sitepoint.com/forums/
[2] http://www.sitepoint.com/forums/forumdisplay.php?f=45

The SitePoint Newsletters

In addition to books like this one, SitePoint publishes free email newsletters, such as *SitePoint Design View*, *SitePoint Market Watch*, and *SitePoint Tech Times*, to name a few. In them, you'll read about the latest news, product releases, trends, tips, and techniques for all aspects of web development. Sign up to one or more SitePoint newsletters at http://www.sitepoint.com/newsletter/.

Your Feedback

If you're unable to find an answer through the forums, or if you wish to contact us for any other reason, the best place to write is books@sitepoint.com. We have a well-staffed email support system set up to track your inquiries, and if our support team members are unable to answer your question, they'll send it straight to us. Suggestions for improvements, as well as notices of any mistakes you may find, are especially welcome.

Conventions Used in This Book

You'll notice that we've used certain typographic and layout styles throughout this book to signify different types of information. Look out for the following items:

Tips, Notes, and Warnings

Hey, You!

Tips will give you helpful little pointers.

Ahem, Excuse Me ...

Notes are useful asides that are related—but not critical—to the topic at hand. Think of them as extra tidbits of information.

Make Sure You Always ...

... pay attention to these important points.

Watch Out!

Warnings will highlight any gotchas that are likely to trip you up along the way.

Acknowledgements

Brandon Eley

Thank-you to my wife Tracy, and our children Peyton and Ellis for their love and understanding when I was working late on this book. Thank-you to my parents, Mike and Karen Eley, my sister Michaela Pennebaker, and all my extended family, friends, and Kappa Sigma Brothers; without you guys I would never leave the office!

Thank-you to my good friend Patrick O'Keefe for advice, wisdom, and encouragement. Thank-you to Shayne Tilley, Chris Wyness, and all of the SitePoint team for the opportunity to share my knowledge—after 8 years as a member of the SitePoint community, I'm unable to think of a better company to work with on my first book. Thanks to Brant Kelsey for inspiring me to set ambitious goals, and to everyone at Kelsey Advertising and Design for their support. Thanks to the many longtime clients that have put up with me all these years. Thanks to Neil Moncrief for coming up with the crazy idea of selling large size shoes online, otherwise I might never have made it into this at all.

Shayne Tilley

Thank-you to my fiancée Justine for being so patient as late nights became early mornings in the creation of this book. Thank-you to my co-author Brandon, mate—you've helped turn this book into something really special. To the editors Raena, Kelly, and Chris—thank-you for your support and supreme skill in turning my rants into a coherent flow of wisdom.

Finally, thankyou to the leadership team at SitePoint: Mark Harbottle, Luke Cuthbertson, and Matt Mickiewicz. Without your support, leadership, advice, and sound direction, this book would have never seen the light of day. I hope you're proud of this monster we created.

The Changing Face of Marketing

Online marketing can be simply defined as promotional activity on the Internet, including email. It can take many forms, including search engine marketing, email marketing, online advertising, social media, and affiliate marketing. This book will dedicate a chapter to each of the core disciplines vital to implementing a successful online marketing plan. We'll cover what's important in building a long-term, stable, and profitable online business, using tried and tested techniques, as well as some of the newest approaches.

Before you jump in and get your hands dirty, there are some overarching principles of online marketing that you need to appreciate before you embark on your first campaign. If you're already an experienced marketer, some of these principles may contradict a few of the old traditional marketing laws that you live by today, so strap yourself in—you're about to see the Internet in a whole new light.

Why is Online Marketing So Important?

If you've ever had formal training in marketing there's a good chance you've already heard about the four Ps. The Ps represent the core considerations of any marketing mix:

1. Product: the actual item for sale, whether it's a physical product, or a service
2. Price: the amount charged for your product—not necessarily monetary
3. Place: where the product or service can be purchased
4. Promotion: how people will find out about the product or service, for example, advertising

The four Ps are good to keep in the back of your mind when building your own marketing strategy, but shouldn't completely dictate your plan. The reason why is simple: there's a key ingredient missing, one very important consideration that will ultimately influence all other aspects of your marketing mix … *people*.

It's All About the People

People will decide if they like your product or not. People will assess if it's value for money. People will determine where they'll choose to spend their money. People will consider when to give promotions a second thought. It's with people in mind that we can start to understand why online marketing is so valuable for a modern marketing mix.

For some time the market has been gradually changing in the way it prefers to consume products and information. The perception that the Web is "just for geeks" is from an era long gone. The mainstream market is hungry for online goods and responding to advertising stimuli right now. If you fail to adapt your approach to marketing, keeping a step ahead of your consumers and competitors, they'll leave you in their wake.

Technical, Fast, and Complex

There are some technical aspects of online marketing that you ought to be aware of—like how Google reads and indexes a web site, new and unusual ways to view the Internet, and the implications of Microsoft launching a new version of Internet Explorer. You'll quickly learn that the Internet can look quite different on another person's browser, and that speed and agility can be your best friend and your worst nightmare. But it's all good news—really! The acronyms may differ, and the technological challenge might be putting you outside your comfort zone, but when you pare back all the layers the key fundamentals for success are still the same. You just need to find the right triggers for your own online audience.

Beyond the Web Geeks

One of the biggest misconceptions about online marketing is that you need to be a web geek in order to succeed. The reality is that some of the best online marketers in the world would struggle to know their PHP from their HTML. What they're good at is identifying customer needs, creating a product to fill that need, attracting those customers to a web site, and converting them into sales. In some ways, a lack of technical knowledge can be more of a bonus than a limitation: You're focused on finding the best possible solution for potential and existing customers—rather than making life easy for web designers and developers—so sacrificing nothing in the act of pleasing your customers.

There are a rare few, who get both web development and online marketing. What makes them special is that they're able to look at marketing and customer opportunities, and translate them perfectly into a design or piece of application development. If you're already a web geek and are hoping to pick up some marketing skills—with this book, you'll be well on the way to achieving success in both fields.

Starting Your Online Journey

When embarking on your own online journey, there are potentially two starting points.

Starting a New Business

You might have created the next million-dollar idea and need to develop a business from scratch. These types of programs are often referred to as web **start-ups** and more and more are popping up each day. When allocating money for a start-up program you'll need a larger budget than an established business, particularly in the PR and brand management elements of your program. Realize that you're a newbie in a global economy and nobody knows you, so you need to develop your credibility and your audience from scratch. It will take time and effort.

Expanding an Existing Business

The other common starting point for online marketing activity is the extension of an existing business into the online space. You may be a small retailer of products to a local market but wish to increase revenue by extending your reach globally. Under this model there are certain benefits you can capitalize on. Your existing customer base can migrate to your online operation (if it's their preference), while processes like fulfilment are already defined. You'll also have a solid customer history, including feedback and testimonials. When launching an online marketing initiative from an existing business, it's important that you leverage these benefits. Include your regular customers in your online campaigns. Use what works well in your offline promotions and transform them into high-performing online campaigns. Grab whatever competitive advantage you can and run with it.

Easy as 1, 2, 3

There are three simple steps to online marketing that help shape every campaign you run. This is regardless of whether it's a PR campaign, email strategy, or advertising initiative—it needs to fit in with the following easy principles.

Attract

A lot of your marketing efforts will focus on attracting visitors to your web site. You need to run campaigns that focus on delivering quality traffic, rather than live under the misconception that more is better.

Engage

Once a visitor arrives, how are you going to keep them coming back for more? Newsletters, RSS feeds, and community development are some examples we'll cover in more detail on how to engage your audience.

Transact

So you have the visitors and they're interested in your message. But it's all for nothing if the **transaction**—the result you're after—fails to occur. A transaction could be a product purchase, a phone call, a newsletter subscription, or a competition entry.

Why You'll Love Online Marketing

Online marketing can deliver a number of great opportunities that are missing in traditional marketing endeavors.

Results Are Instantaneous

When you fire off your first email campaign, activate your first advertising promotion, or try any of the other ideas you learn in this book, you'll see almost instant results. Waiting for snail mail will be relegated to the past, as will waiting up for that 2.00 a.m. TV ad. As soon as you act, you'll see results.

New Levels of Customer Interaction

You may already interact with friends and family on sites like Facebook[1] or MySpace.[2] This book will show you how to interact and socialize on behalf of your business with your customers—actual and potential—online. You'll find out how to communicate and develop strong customer loyalty without them even having heard your voice.

A Team Player

Online marketing plays well with conventional areas of marketing. Campaigns are flexible and able to accommodate core brand values. It can be used in conjunction with traditional direct marketing and awareness campaigns, as well as performing well on its own.

Instant Global Market

The barrier of location is gone. Some of your most profitable long-term customers might be halfway around the world, and contacting them is now a cinch! Your business might be unsuitable for a global market, and that's okay—but if the opposite is true, your reach explodes overnight.

---

[1] http://facebook.com/
[2] http://myspace.com/

Opportunities Are Everywhere

Opportunities are plentiful in the brave new world of online marketing. Creative thinkers right now are finding new ways to take their products and services to markets that are completely untapped. In each chapter of this book, we'll take you through all the fundamentals of online marketing and show you tactics that work.

Embrace trying a new approach. How quick you are can influence how successful your campaigns will be. For example, some of Twitter's most popular users now have audiences that are the envy of big business—all because they were brave enough to try a new strategy. These entrepreneurs looked at the potential of the opportunity, rather than its proven viability.

Start Me Up!

You now should have a good understanding of what online marketing is and why it's an important part of a modern business's marketing mix. You're now ready to roll up your sleeves and start building some online campaigns of your own.

21st Century Public Relations and Media

The marketing landscape has changed dramatically in recent years. The reliance on the mainstream media to break stories about companies and products is waning, while the number of press releases grows daily. It's increasingly difficult for small and medium-sized businesses to gain mainstream coverage from conventional media forms. So, rather than narrow their focus towards journalists in the hope of hitting the publishing jackpot, small and medium-sized companies are now producing press statements that target web site publishers and bloggers relevant to their niche, as well as targeting customers directly.

To understand the new rules of pubic relations and media, we must first take a look at the days before electronic communication became dominant. When the print media ruled the roost, well before the Internet was even thought of, there were two major ways companies promoted new products and services: by advertising, or through editorial coverage. Public relations used to be something of a secret art, and only the most seasoned and experienced PR people could break their story in the news. It was as much about having a relationship with that key reporter as it was about writing fantastic marketing copy.

In this chapter we'll explore public relations, and discuss the ways we can use promotional opportunities and press releases so that your company is mentioned on web sites, blogs, and online communities. We'll also look at how to use blogs and non-traditional marketing techniques to place your brand in front of millions of people.

What is Public Relations?

Public relations—or PR, for short—is the practice of managing the public image of a company, organization, or person. PR consists of managing the flow of information and news between a person, company, or organization and the public. Until recently, the main conduit for disseminating information about a company or product was the press release. Today, company web sites, blogs, and even social media services serve as viable channels for companies to speak to the public.

Press Releases

A **press release** or news release is an official statement sent to media outlets providing detailed information about an event the company wants to get into the news, such as a new product launch or investor relations.

Press releases date back to the early 1900s and came about as a way for companies to mitigate bad publicity. Before advances in communications allowed us access to both sides of the story, it was common for newspapers to print stories about an accident or harmful event before having all the facts. Companies began sending statements to the newspapers as a way to *set the record straight*—a sort of preemptive strike, if you like.

As public relations evolved, companies (or their public relations agencies) crafted carefully worded press releases and sent them to a handful of influential reporters in the hope their story would be published in a newspaper or magazine. If it was published, they'd receive great publicity. And if not ... well, that was the bad part. Most press releases failed to gain that prized media coverage.

Press Releases in the 21st Century

With all these exciting new developments in online marketing, you might be thinking, "I can publish news to my web site—why should I send out a press release?" Companies still send press releases because they're an effective way to spread the word about your company. Press releases, when written and distributed efficiently, can strengthen brand awareness, increase sales, and generate buzz about your company and products.

Today, press releases are used widely. As well as being sent to mainstream media journalists, press releases are now available online for customers to find through a web search, or read on a company's blog. Many bloggers and online publishers access these to read for story ideas close to their niche.

You can also use press releases to communicate directly to your customers, as well as bloggers, writers, and other key players in your industry. Press releases can be an incredibly effective medium for you to publish news and information about your company, products, or services.

When to Write a Press Release

Start now! You simply cannot write too many press releases. Okay, that might be a bit of a stretch, but that's the mindset you should have about it. You should write press releases anytime you have news or information to share to your customers, clients, or investors. If you would post it to your web site's News section, then it probably deserves a press release.

The following are all excellent reasons why you'd send a press release:

- a new product or service to announce
- a case study about how you helped a client or made a client money
- a new employee has been hired with extensive experience in your industry
- your company has won an award or been recognized in your industry as a thought leader
- your company, product, or service was reviewed favorably
- it's a communication requirement for investor relations (quarterly financial reports for public companies)

Anatomy of a Press Release

In the old days, press releases were specially formatted and provided reporters with only the most pertinent information that the company felt they needed. Because releases were sent mostly to reporters with experience in a specific industry, they often used technical jargon and industry-specific terminology without explanation or background information. Today's press releases talk to many audiences—your customers, bloggers, reporters, investors—so you need to make sure that your language and terminology is widely accessible, and that you're not overestimating their level of knowledge in that area. Think back to your sixth grade English class and answer the who, what, when, where, why, and how of your story.

What Should You Include In Your Press Release?

Your press release should engage readers, so be sure to include supporting media whenever appropriate to help your customers understand your content. Think of a popular news source like CNN—as well as text, their articles feature photos, videos, and quotes to keep the reader's interest and help tell the story. When writing your press release, try to include any information that will help support your message, such as:

- quotes from the president, owner, or other key personnel and industry experts
- customer testimonials
- product reviews
- awards and other examples of industry recognition
- offers or calls to action

Offer supporting evidence when making marketing claims. If you say your product is the best, you need to support the claim with third-party reviews, specifications, or some kind of data. Similarly, if you hire a new employee or win an award, describe how that will positively affect your business. Did you just hire a hotshot away from a competitor? Did you win an award showing your expertise in a certain area? How does that help your clients or customers? How does it impact on them?

Press Releases on Steroids!

Press releases are rarely sent by facsimile these days. When a press release is posted online, it's immediately available and has all the capabilities of a regular web page.

Use the benefits of hypertext to your advantage, and include as much supporting material as possible.

Hyperlinks

Link key phrases and calls to action to appropriate landing pages on your web site. This will allow your customers to place an order or sign up if interested, and it's also excellent for search engines. These links to your web site will appear everywhere the press release is published, which, if you use a newswire, could be a lot of places. Those incoming links will help you rank on search engines for the phrases that are hyperlinked.

Photos

Adding photos can make an ordinary press release stand out from the crowd. If you're advertising a new product, make sure to include a product photograph. If you hired a new employee, make sure their photograph is included.

Audio

Consider adding audio clips of interviews, podcast excerpts, or quotes featured in the press release.

Video

When appropriate, videos can add an extra dimension never before available in press releases. Videos of product reviews, demonstrations, or interviews are excellent additions to a press release.

Social Media Facilities

Adding buttons to post the item to popular social bookmarking sites like Digg,[1] Delicious,[2] and Technorati[3] can help publicize the press release. As people use social media to bookmark or share your release, it will be exposed to their friends, helping the news spread even further.

---

[1] http://digg.com/
[2] http://delicious.com/
[3] http://technorati.com/

How Long Should My Press Release Be?

Before you concern yourself with length, you should focus on content. Your press release should adequately cover the topic you're writing about. You should only be concerned with whether your press release is long enough after you've covered all the details. Once you've done that, it's time to review the length of your press release.

Your press release should be relatively short at 400–500 words. If it's much longer, you risk losing your audience's attention. Any shorter, and your story might be too short to cover all the important details. Also, remember that journalists and bloggers searching for information to write about want enough information to decide whether to cover the story, without being required to read a novel.

Once you've written your release, if you find that it's less than 400 words, consider adding a quote or more supporting information. Did you answer the important facts: the who, what, when, where, why, and how? If your release is longer than 600 words, review the release to see if you can make your message more concise. Remove any fluff and technical jargon that's unnecessary. As William Strunk, Jr. explains in *The Elements of Style*:[4]

> Omit needless words. Vigorous writing is concise. A sentence should contain no unnecessary words, a paragraph no unnecessary sentences, for the same reason that a drawing should have no unnecessary lines and a machine no unnecessary parts. This requires not that the writer make all his sentences short, or that he avoid all detail and treat his subjects only in outline, but that every word tell.

When It's Okay To Exclude "For Immediate Release"

In printed press releases, the phrase "For Immediate Release" was used to inform reporters they could publish your story immediately. Sometimes, if the news was intended to be released at a specific time in the future, press releases included a "Do not publish before ..." statement. If you upload your press release to the Web, this statement is unnecessary—it's already published.

---

[4] Boston: Allyn and Bacon, 2000

Official Format

Effective press releases have a consistent format. Here's how to put one together.

Headline   This should be a short, engaging title that draws in your reader.

Summary   Sum up the entire press release in two or three short sentences. Engage the reader and give them enough information to adequately comprehend the news in the release.

Location and Dateline The location and date of your release should immediately precede the body.

Body   Expand on the summary, provide facts and figures, and add quotes. You can embed photos and videos in the body.

About You   Briefly describe your company and its services or products.

Media Contact Information You should always include contact information—you could choose to put these near the top of the release, but my advice is to include it at the bottom. If your reader has taken the time to read through to the end of your release, chances are they were interested. Make sure to include contact information here so they can access additional information if needed.

Closing   Three hash or pound symbols—###—signal the close of the press release and are typically centered on the page.

Press Release Writing Services

If you're short on time, or just think your content leaves a little to be desired, there are services that will write your press release for you for a nominal fee. Many press release distribution schemes offer writing services—we'll discuss these in the section called "Using an Online Newswire." You could also hire a copywriter, either locally or by using a service such as eLance.[5] When using a copywriter, make sure they have experience writing press releases, and ask for several examples.

Stand Out from the Crowd

With so many press releases sent out every day, you need to stand out to be noticed. The first step is to follow the advice above in creating a compelling, well-formatted press release and submitting it where it can gain the widest exposure. But that's still a bit limited. How can you almost guarantee your press release will be written about in a blog, web site, or newspaper?

Make It Easy

Make it easy for publishers, bloggers, and journalists to publish your story by doing some of their work for them. Provide them with a media kit—a package of information about your company or organization. Media kits often contain:

- high-resolution logo in multiple formats
- a company profile and history
- executive biographies with head shots
- product or service information with product photos

Be sure to include multiple formats for all graphics. Include print-quality and web-quality graphics for use in multiple media formats. Providing a vector version of your logo, such as the Encapsulated PostScript Format (EPS), will ensure that the publisher can display your logo correctly regardless of what size it's rendered.

Be Available

Even with a well-crafted press release, a journalist may need to ask you a question, or may want to interview you or key staff at your company for their story. Be sure

---

[5] http://elance.com/

to include a media contact, and include multiple ways to reach them. At a minimum, you should include your:

- office phone number
- mobile phone number
- email address

Distribute Press Releases

Do you still use a fax machine? In the old days, you would fax your press release to journalists. You might send a release to five or ten journalists that specialized in your niche, hoping one would pick up the story. The press release would go out on *the wire*, meaning it was sent by telegraph, or later by fax. They still call it a news-wire, but sending press releases in the 21st century requires far fewer trees.

There are several ways to send your press release, but the most popular are email (directly to journalists), online newswire, and company web site uploads. We'll discuss each in a little more detail.

Emailing Journalists Directly

Email can be very effective at targeting your press release to specific bloggers or journalists. By emailing them individually, you increase the chance they'll actually read your release.

Your email's subject line should be short and informative. Condense your press release headline into five to ten words and engage the reader with the most important information from your press release.

When emailing a blogger or journalist, address them and their publication by name in the body or title of the email. For instance, your introduction might read "Press Release for Michael Arrington, TechCrunch." Personally addressing the recipient will show them that you didn't just spray your press release at a few hundred (or thousand) email addresses.

Want to go the extra mile? Include a short, personal introduction and explanation of why the story is a good fit for their publication. Was there a similar product or service covered by the publication in the past? A short introduction can lend a personal touch to your email, but keep it short. And avoid presuming to know what they'll like or want to publish.

With the volume of computer viruses these days, unwanted email attachments are rarely opened. Instead, paste the text of your press release directly into the email. If they are interested in your story, they will respond asking for supporting documents, such as photos and videos. Make sure to list any supporting information available, such as quotes, photos, videos, or a PDF release. Also, if you've uploaded the entire press release to your web site, be sure to include a link at the bottom of your email.

Using an Online Newswire

Online newswires are the newest and most effective way to have your press release read by interested journalists, publishers, bloggers, and customers. Newswires have been around for ages, but their press releases were only available to journalists or companies that subscribed to them. Today, newswires publish press releases on their web sites, and submit them to services such as Google News and Yahoo, making them instantly available to your customers who are searching the Internet.

Newswires also offer direct distribution to journalists and publications looking for your news. By offering **RSS**—Really Simple Syndication—feeds for specific searches and industries, publishers can subscribe to receive new press releases automatically as they become available. RSS feeds are a standardized format for received updates from a web site or news source. To view updates, you can use an RSS reader, such as Google Reader,[6] or your email client.

Paid PR Newswires

- PRWeb—http://prweb.com/
- eReleases—http://ereleases.com/
- Marketwire—http://marketwire.com/
- Business Wire—http://businesswire.com/

---

[6] http://google.com/reader

Free Newswires

- PR.com—http://pr.com/
- PRLog—http://prlog.org/
- 24-7 Press Release—http://24-7pressrelease.com/
- 1888 Press Release—http://1888pressrelease.com/
- ClickPress—http://clickpress.com/
- PR LEAP—http://prleap.com/

As with everything, you get what you pay for. The free and low-cost services don't have the same distribution channels the paid services have, and often lack features such as the ability to embed hyperlinks and videos. Paid services often have the following advantages:

- distribution through the Associated Press in the US (making your release available to all major newspapers and media outlets)
- greater number of targeted industry niches the release is sent to
- social media options, such as social bookmarking links or posts to Twitter
- search engine optimization via anchor text links and other HTML tags

Posting to Your Web Site

In addition to emailing your press release or using online newswires, you should post your press releases to your company web site. It adds relevant content to your web site and will often help your site appear higher in search engines before other sources, cutting out the middleman.

Press releases are often posted to a media or press section of a company's web site. Make sure that your press releases are easy to find, especially from your homepage.

Use Blogs to Spread the Word

In January, 2009, US Airways Flight 1549 experienced an engine failure after flying through a flock of geese. Captain Chesley "Sully" Sullenberger had to think quickly—unable to make it back to the airport, the pilot made the tough decision to attempt an emergency landing in the Hudson River. Several years ago, the news would have been broken by reporters from helicopters or news vans—but that day, a pedestrian in the area snapped a photo on his iPhone and posted it to the microblogging service, Twitter.[7] Within just a few minutes, news had spread through the blogosphere[8] to make its way to the mainstream media. So many reporters mentioned or linked to the picture that the TwitPic service, where the image was stored, went down temporarily. The original tweet and photo are still viewable on Twitter[9].

Traditional media still exists, but your greatest coverage might come from a 16-year-old kid in a garage. In the interconnected world we live in, anyone can break a story. You don't have to witness a crash-landing in the Hudson to attract traffic to your web site. There are private blogs with a readership as large as some major metropolitan newspapers. TechCrunch,[10] a private blog network founded by Michael Arrington, claims on its advertising page to reach over 5,000,000 readers per month.[11]

There are major blogs like TechCrunch in almost every industry and niche. Let's look at how to find them and use them to your advantage.

Find Influential Blogs and Web Sites

Knowing the influential blogs and web sites in your niche is the first step in spreading the word. Using search engines and directories, you can find web sites and blogs related to your company, product, or service.

Blog-specific search engines, like Technorati[12] and Google Blog Search,[13] and directories like AllTop,[14] are great for finding blogs related to your niche. Also utilize regular search engines for other web sites, as well as online publications and communities that may use an alternative label to "blogs." Try search queries that include the name of your niche, industry, or products, as well as words like *community*, *news*, or *blog*.

When you find popular web sites covering your niche, it's a great idea to subscribe to their RSS feeds where available and keep up with the topics they write about.

---

[7] http://twitter.com/

[8] http://techcrunch.com/2009/01/15/plane-crashes-in-hudson-first-pictures-on-flickr-tumblr-twitpic/

[9] http://twitpic.com/135xa

[10] http://techcrunch.com/

[11] http://techcrunch.com/advertise/

[12] http://technorati.com/

[13] http://blogsearch.google.com/

[14] http://alltop.com/

Comment on Influential Blogs

Commenting on influential blogs is a marketing strategy in itself. If you can provide value to the blog by commenting, you'll be seen as an asset to the community and can establish yourself as an expert in your field. In the future, if the blogger should come across a story about you or your company, they'll already be familiar with you and be more likely to cover the story.

When to Comment

Before commenting on blogs or online communities, ask yourself this simple question: "Can I answer a question or add value here?" If the answer is yes, consider leaving a comment. It's a poor idea to post a comment just to place your name or web address on a blog. Make sure you're adding value, otherwise you're just wasting time instead of building your online reputation or helping the web site's readers.

How to Comment

Post advice in a friendly, personal style. Address the post's author or other commenters directly, offering your feedback or advice. Posting criticisms or negative feedback is acceptable, but be professional and articulate your point using references.

Cite third-party references and examples *at least* as much as linking to your own web site. It's important that you make your point, rather than advertise your company or products.

Danger! When to Avoid Commenting

If a blogger or commenter personally attacks you or your company, think twice before responding. Often, commenting will only add gasoline to the flame, making an already bad situation worse. Instead, wait a while and see how it's received. You'd be surprised how often a customer or employee will come to your defense. Letting a third party counter the attack could defuse the situation before it goes awry.

Send Your Press Releases Directly to Influential Bloggers

Sending press releases to blogs is a great way to spread your message even further. Refer to the list of influential blogs you compiled earlier from the section called "Find Influential Blogs and Web Sites" for suitable leads.

Make It Personal

When contacting individual bloggers, start with a personalized email (see the previous section on sending press releases by email).

Look on their web site for information on how to pitch to them. Many blogs have instructions on how they wish to be pitched, and may have a dedicated email address for pitches.

Doing your research here can really pay off. Influential bloggers and journalists are often inundated with email pitches. Sending to the wrong email address or in the wrong format could mean being deleted immediately. As blogger Josh Catone says in his SitePoint article, How To Pitch a Blogger:[15] "Bloggers are a busy bunch and we generally like to put as much of our time and effort as possible into actual research or writing. If the phone is ringing non-stop all day, it cuts into our writing time."

If you're unable to find a dedicated email address or contact information on the web site, consider sending an email to the general contact email address. Ask for the correct information for sending pitches and press releases.

Build a List

You'll likely be sending press releases to the same bloggers and journalists again and again. Start building a list of media contacts, with notes about the types of press releases they're interested in.

As you write more and more press releases, you'll find that sending them will become easier as your list grows and requires less and less research up front.

---

[15] http://sitepoint.com/blogs/2008/07/12/how-to-pitch-a-blogger/

Smaller Blogs Copy Bigger Blogs

You might think that once the big sites cover a news story, it simply fades away. You might be surprised to know that smaller blogs follow large, influential blogs and often write about interesting stories in their own blogs, creating a link back to your site. Some blogging tools use a special kind of link called a **ping** or **track-back**—an automated notification to a site to inform the owner that you linked to one of their blog entries.

With pings or trackbacks enabled on your blog, when another blogger links to a blog entry on your web site, a comment will be placed in the entry on your blog, linking back to their blog. These can provide an additional traffic source to smaller blogs.

Non-traditional Marketing

Non-traditional marketing, sometimes called guerilla marketing, is a blanket term that covers all kinds of unconventional marketing strategies that usually spread through **word of mouth**—or simply, people talking to their friends. Non-traditional marketing existed before the Internet was around, but the interconnected Web allows for faster, almost instant, spreading of a message to thousands or millions of people.

Viral marketing refers to the exponential spreading of a marketing message, like a virus. It's the effect word of mouth can have on an ad, campaign, or even just a video. Non-traditional marketing is all about using unconventional tactics to spread the word about a company or product, often on a small budget (or smaller than with a traditional advertising campaign).

Non-traditional Marketing Offline

Wait a minute—this is a book about *online* marketing, right? Indeed it is, but there's still a lot we can learn from offline marketing tactics and apply to our online efforts. Let's take a look at them.

Environmental Marketing

Graffiti on signs, park benches with messages on them, and painted manhole covers are all examples of environmental marketing. Environmental marketing places a form of message in an unexpected place, designed purely to be noticed.

There have been some excellent examples of environmental marketing, such as US takeaway chain Chick-fil-A's "Eat Mor Chikin" campaign,[16] in which cows stand on water towers and billboards, holding up signs which implore passers-by to eat chicken instead of cows.

Endorsements

When a celebrity wears a particular brand of clothes or jewelry, people notice. Companies often give products to celebrities in the hope they'll use them in public, as unofficial celebrity endorsements are just as effective at impacting sales too.

Influence and Word of Mouth

Hush Puppies was a struggling shoe company leading into 1994. Their sales had dwindled to 100,000 pairs a year and Wolverine, Hush Puppies' parent company, was considering dropping the brand. Then a few influential people were spotted wearing them in New York City, and suddenly young people eagerly sought out the comfortable, casual shoes. They rummaged in small shoe stores all over Manhattan to score a pair.

The phenomenon thrust Hush Puppies back on the scene, where sales grew to over 11.5 million pairs in just two years. They appeared on popular TV shows such as *Melrose Place*[17] and were worn by actor Tom Hanks in the movie *Forrest Gump*.[18] Hush Puppies took advantage of their popularity, sending free pairs to celebrities and fashion moguls. They capitalized on their new-found success, launching an advertising campaign that featured Hush Puppies on young people looking casual and relaxed.

You can find out more about Hush Puppies' success in an article from the *Los Angeles Times*,[19] or visit the Hush Puppies web site.[20]

---

[16] http://chick-fil-a.com/#thecows
[17] http://imdb.com/title/tt0103491/
[18] http://imdb.com/title/tt0109830/
[19] http://articles.latimes.com/1997/aug/30/business/fi-27351
[20] http://hushpuppies.com/

Shock Marketing

Paying a person to tattoo the name of your business on their forehead or run streaking through a football game will probably attract attention—though whether it's the type of marketing you want to represent your brand is debatable. Shock marketing relies mostly on outlandish stunts that shock or offend people to garner attention. Using bold, controversial ads or scantily clad models to promote your web site would be examples of shock marketing online.

Undercover Marketing

Hiring people to impersonate customers is known as undercover marketing, and should be avoided. Whether you're hiring actors to line up waiting for a product launch or post a positive review on Amazon,[21] undercover marketing is almost always exposed. It could be effective if it remains undetected, but it's never worth the risk of damaging your brand.

Homemade videos can sometimes fall into this category, if the video is produced for the purpose of marketing, but passed off as an original or customer-created work.

Urban Legend

Creating an urban legend is easier said than done. The hype surrounding *The Blair Witch Project* movie is an excellent example of word-of-mouth hype generated by inventing an urban legend.[22] The combination of the movie's low budget and rumors purporting that there was some truth to the story created a buzz that generated a huge amount of interest in the movie, even after the hoax was revealed—and thus millions of dollars in ticket sales.

Non-traditional Marketing Online

We can adopt a number of good principles from offline marketing in our online campaigns.

---

[21] http://amazon.com/

[22] *The Blair Witch Project* [http://en.wikipedia.org/wiki/The_Blair_Witch_Project]

Tell a Story

Non-traditional marketing is about telling a story or delivering a message. It might be funny, shocking, or amazing. It might be a video, a blog post, or a Twitter message (a tweet). The key is to create an idea that is consistent with your brand and who you are as a company.

First, think of the message you want to convey. What is unique or unusual about your product or service? Is there a quirky aspect of your company that people can identify with?

Everyone Loves to Laugh

Using humor is a great way to attract attention to your brand.

Will it Blend?[23] is one of the most successful non-traditional marketing campaigns in recent years. Tom Dickson, founder of Blendtec—makers of high-end blenders—posted a video series. The videos feature Tom blending items such as an iPhone, "diamonds" (really cubic zirconias), a rake handle, and a Chuck Norris figurine. The iPhone video has been watched over six million times. The videos increased brand awareness, and sales for Blendtec blenders shot up 40% in 2006, the year they launched the campaign.

The *Will it Blend?* videos' success was relatively unplanned. In an article for the *Wall Street Journal*,[24] George Wright, Blendtec's marketing director, said, "I knew … we wanted to do YouTube. Initially, we were thinking this might be a tool our sales force could use to show how robust our equipment is as part of their training. Quite frankly, if that's all we achieved from that campaign, I would have considered it successful." The initial video series cost the company $US50 to produce.

Will it Blend is a great example of how you can be light-hearted and yet create an amazing marketing tool for your business. Blendtec sells high-end blenders—top of the line consumer and professional models. Yet they were able to build brand awareness by creating hilarious videos that showed them blending wacky items, as well as proving the durability of their products. If it could blend an iPhone, then a smoothie would be a piece of cake!

---

[23] http://youtube.com/user/Blendtec

[24] http://online.wsj.com/article/SB118330775119654449.html

Can You Plan to Go Viral?

The *Will it Blend?* videos were a viral phenomenon inadvertently. They were only created to show how durable their products were, and hopefully make people smile. One of the most common misconceptions about non-traditional marketing is that you *can* plan for a campaign to "go viral."

While you can plan the campaign, it's purely up to chance whether it will go viral. The best advice is to create unique and interesting content and put it out there. It may or may not go viral, but it can be a great representation of your brand, nonetheless.

There are advertising agencies that specialize in creating viral marketing campaigns. Does it work? Sometimes. Agencies specializing in guerilla marketing can be effective at projecting the word about your business, but there are some caveats.

Words of Wisdom

If you're planning a guerilla marketing campaign, there are some things you should consider.

First, and most importantly, be genuine. It's a poor idea to present yourself or your company as different to what you really are, or to try and trick the public into believing an untruth. The Web is full of amateur investigative reporters who would love to break a story, leading to bad publicity.

Second, be sure to obey any applicable laws and, naturally, stay away from dangerous activities. This should go without saying, but think through the potential outcomes of your campaign. There are lots of interesting ways to draw attention to your company, so legal trouble should be avoided.

Be smart with your campaigns and have fun with them, but be careful of going overboard just to garner some free publicity. Find ways to involve your customers, such as creating contests where users submit homemade videos or produce a creative idea.

The Bomb Squad: Ultimate Bad Press

In 2007, guerrilla marketing agency, Interference, Inc. placed small, magnetic, electronic lights all around several metropolitan cities. The devices were intended to promote *Aqua Teen Hunger Force*,[25] an animated television show by Adult Swim and Cartoon Network. The signs caused a bomb scare in Boston, where bridges and roads were closed while bomb squads were brought in to investigate. One of the devices was even destroyed by explosive as a precaution.

The publicity stunt resulted in extremely bad publicity for Cartoon Network and Adult Swim, and several people who distributed the signs were arrested. The potential danger of affixing electronic devices underneath bridges should have been obvious! You can read about this failed campaign in a story at CNN.[26]

Selling the Owner on Online Marketing

If you're not the decision maker at your company, you may have a hard time selling new marketing techniques to the "powers that be."

While it's critically important to maintain your brand, PR and legal departments (and even the owner) can sometimes obstruct online marketing efforts by trying to screen every piece of information that goes out of a company. What can you do to encourage everyone in your company to be on board?

Educate Your Colleagues

The first step is to educate them—why not show them what you've learned from this book? Schedule a meeting to present what you've learned from this book. Show them that trying a new concept can still involve presenting a consistent brand image. Assure them that company policies and procedures can still be followed, even when using social media or posting content online.

Provide Examples

The best way to prove the benefits of social media is to show them some examples. By presenting articles or case studies from prominent publications, you can showcase how other companies have used online marketing to grow their business.

---

[25] http://imdb.com/title/tt0297494/

[26] http://edition.cnn.com/2007/US/01/31/boston.bombscare/index.html

Work within Company Policies

Your company is likely to have policies in place like nondisclosure and confidentiality agreements. Your organization probably already has a code of conduct that all employees are expected to abide by. Many organizations are beginning to address social media use as part of these policies. If your company has yet to adopt a social media policy, drafting one could help higher-ups feel comfortable letting employees and departments branch out to social media. Instead of dictating where and how employees can post or what type of messages they can post, start by reaffirming what types of behavior are acceptable or unacceptable.

Reinforce existing policies. For instance, remind employees that nondisclosure agreements and confidentiality agreements still apply. Let employees know how they should conduct themselves when acting on behalf of the company. The same applies online.

The Greteman Group, a branding agency, has a great example of a blogging and social media policy on their blog.[27] It asks that employees refrain from letting their personal use of social media interfere with their billable time, but it also recognizes the value that these activities can bring to their business, and encourages smart use of social networks and blogging for business purposes.

Modern Monitoring of Press Coverage

When a journalist writes about your company after reading your press release, you want to know about it! Monitoring the news channels is an important part of public relations. Whether it's good or bad, it's necessary to keep tabs on what people are saying about your company and your products or services.

Monitoring press coverage used to be expensive, because monitoring newspapers and radio was complicated and error-prone. Technology has come a long way, fortunately, and monitoring the Internet for your company and personal brand is easier than ever. Below, I'll give you a strategy for effectively monitoring press coverage, including any mention of your company, trademarks, or key employees.

---

[27] http://gretemangroup.com/blog/index.php/2009/01/social-media-policy/

What Should You Track?

The first step in monitoring your brand is determining what you want to monitor! It's a lot like keyword research. There are several areas you may want to consider tracking, including:

- your company name
- key employees' names
- trademarks you own
- competitor names
- key search engine phrases (phrases you want to rank well for in search engines, such as your product names, web site name, company name, and so on)

What you monitor is really up to you. You may only want to know when someone writes about you, but I personally like to know when my competitor receives press coverage too!

RSS (Really Simple Syndication)

RSS, or Really Simple Syndication, is a way to keep track of web sites without having to actually visit them. When you visit most web sites, typically blogs or search engines, you'll see a link or button that's labeled Subscribe, Feed, RSS, RSS Feed, or similar. This link is a feed of web site updates or search results and is updated automatically when the web site is updated.

To use RSS feeds, you just need to have a feed reader. A popular free online feed reader is Google Reader.[28] Many popular email clients such as Outlook, Apple Mail, and Thunderbird also support RSS feeds directly in your email client.

Once you've set up a feed reader on your computer, clicking an RSS link or button automatically adds that feed to your reader. You can categorize and organize feeds within your reader of choice.

---

[28] http://google.com/reader

Technorati Blog Search

Technorati is a blog search engine. With over 100 million blogs indexed, as well as other social media content, Technorati is an excellent resource that you should track. Fortunately, they make it simple to save searches as RSS feeds.

You can track down mentions of your favorite topics using the main search bar at the Technorati homepage, search for your company name, product name, or the person's name you want to track (if multiple words, be sure to enclose them in quotation marks). On the search results page, click the "Subscribe" link to the right above the "Try filtering your results" bar.

Google Alerts

Google Alerts constantly monitors Google News, Blog Search, Video Search, Groups, and Web Search and notifies you when it finds anything matching your criteria. Set up searches for your company name, key employees (such as the president or owner), and products or trademarks you own. You can ask Google to notify you instantly, daily, or weekly by email, or you can choose to receive the notifications through an RSS feed.

Social Media Monitoring Services

Knowing when your company or product is mentioned in the major news or blogs is only part of the picture. You want to know when *people* mention your product or company! Using a social media monitoring service like Trackur,[29] you can be notified when you're mentioned on sites such as Facebook,[30] Twitter,[31] MySpace,[32] and LinkedIn.[33]

Twitter Search[34] is an excellent way to find out what is going on in the universe of Twitter—the **Twitterverse**. If you just type a word or phrase, you'll see every time it's been mentioned. But what I like about Twitter Search is that you can search for a Twitter user's name by using *@username*, or a hashtag using *#hashtag*. **Hashtags**

---

[29] http://trackur.com/

[30] http://facebook.com/

[31] http://twitter.com/

[32] http://myspace.com/

[33] http://linkedin.com/

[34] http://search.twitter.com/

are a way of tagging topics on social media so that you can see trends and search easier. For instance, if you were tweeting about the South by Southwest conference, the hashtag to use is *#sxsw*.

You can customize Twitter Search by using operators, or words that trigger advanced search options. Using the parameter *from*, you can search for tweets from a specific Twitter user. Likewise, you can search for all tweets except that user by using the "not from" operator: *-from*. For example, *-from:sitepointdotcom sitepoint* would return all Tweets mentioning SitePoint that are not from the SitePoint Twitter account.

Twitter search results can be retrieved using RSS, so it's easy to keep track.

BackType[35] is a service that lets you find, track, and share comments from all over the Internet. Commenting on blogs, social media services, and news sites is a very powerful way of both generating traffic to your web site and creating incoming links for higher search engine ranking. There's no guarantee that commenting will help your search engine rankings, but it will help build your brand and generate traffic to your web site. We'll cover this in detail in Chapter 4.

Now that you have a toolbox of services, how do you use them? Check RSS feeds and emails daily. I have emails filtering to a specified folder automatically so that my inbox remains uncluttered. About once every day or two, I'll go in and browse through them. After sending press releases, I'll monitor these searches extra carefully so that I notice when we've been written about.

Someone Wrote about Me! What Now?

Finding out when and where people are talking about you is only the first part. If they wrote a flattering comment about your company, product, or service, how do you thank them? If it's negative, how do you respond?

Responding to Flattering Press

Of course, the goal of PR is for the media to write about your company, product, or service favorably. With blogs and online communities, you can respond directly to favorable comments. Write a short comment on the post thanking them for mention-

---

[35] http://backtype.com/

ing them. Let them know what you liked best about the article or post, and be sincere. You could even post about it on your own blog if you feel it's appropriate.

Responding to Negative Comments

You need to expect some negative commentary. There will be bad reviews, disagreements with your policies, and other negative comments. You can respond, but I'd advise against being on the defensive. If you disagree with the article or post, be respectful and state your point, and leave it at that.

If the article—or parts of it—are accurate, mention that in your comments. Being honest and truthful about your company will build a lot of credibility with the author and readers.

If anyone raises a question in the comments, respond. The point is to be an active participant.

Be Thankful for the Author's Time

People like their work to receive attention, so responding to a post (good or bad) can mean more press in the future. Always be professional and sincere, and thank the author whenever possible for their time writing about your company or product.

Summary

Public relations has moved on from what it used to be. It's grown and evolved and can be a powerful marketing tool for your business. We've shown how press releases have changed and how they can be used to spread the word about your company and products. We've discussed ways to spread the word through blogs and web sites, and how to use non-traditional advertising. But making your message known is only one part of the puzzle. Be sure to check out Chapter 5 for ways to further spread your brand and increase your online reputation.

For more information on using public relations and press releases to market your business, check out *The New Rules of Marketing & PR* by David Meerman Scott.[36]

---

[36] New Jersey: Wiley, 2007

Turn Page Views into Profit

Throughout this book we're exploring various ways to attract and keep customers, but it's your web site that will convert those visitors into customers and build revenue for your business.

Think of your web site as the foundations of your entire marketing program—a shaky foundation can have disastrous consequences. Your visitors have better things to do with their time than try to interpret confusing language or a difficult design—if your site only serves to baffle them, they'll simply take their money elsewhere. Even if your site receives a million visitors, it's a waste spending time and money on marketing activity if none of them buy anything. The goal is to **make conversions**—that is, turn visitors into customers.

A crisp and professional design can help strengthen user trust and improve your brand representation—but if you sacrifice ease of use in favor of a miniature work of abstract art, this will have a detrimental effect on your web site's income potential. In this chapter we'll explore concepts like accessibility, usability, web browser compatibility, and other issues that can have a significant impact on your traffic and earnings.

While some parts of this chapter will be a little technical, rest assured it's unnecessary for you to understand exactly how a web site is constructed in order to recognize the principles of a high-conversion web site; you just need to be able to provide sound guidance and direction to your design and development teams, and in order to do this, you should have an understanding of some of the issues involved.

Usability

Usability is relatively easy to define: it's the ease with which your users can complete their chosen tasks on your web site. But why is it so important?

At the start of this chapter I touched on the fact that web sites that are presented as works of art can cause problems with usability. The reality is that it's unnecessary to sacrifice aesthetics for usability. Your design should be inherently usable first and foremost, with aesthetics strengthening the customer's experience. When working with your design team, you need to communicate your usability challenges as a problem that needs to be solved with effective design. These are real-world problems and effective design should increase usability, rather than hinder your visitors.

Your users, just like you, only have so much time in the day, and so will only provide you with a limited amount of their attention. And if there's anything that prohibits them from using their time efficiently—like a badly designed web site—then they'll go elsewhere.

Improving Usability: Test Early, Test Often

The important truth about web usability is that the question, "is my site usable?" can really only be answered by your users. The key to finding out is by conducting usability tests, and you can do this at just about every step of the way. Important design decisions are too often made around a meeting room table, with time consuming debates on what people *feel* and *think* is the right thing to do for users. Instead, we should be asking the users themselves throughout the whole design process.

Usability testing is often performed as one of the final stages of the design process—if at all. As deadlines loom, testing is often cut short. But usability tests should commence before the design stage is finished. Running tests throughout the design process helps to refine the project on an ongoing basis, avoiding last-minute, poorly executed testing.

Be aware that comprehensive testing is no guarantee of a more accurate result—as Jakob Nielsen points out,[1] a smaller usability test will reveal most of your usability pitfalls.

Create Use Cases

Use cases describe a set of actions you expect visitors to be able to accomplish on your site. Use cases can form a part of your design specification for the site designers and developers to work from when creating your site, and can be employed for usability testing. They can vary from simple, straightforward tasks to complex interactions with your web site.

For example, a set of simple test cases for an ecommerce web site might describe the following common actions:

- a customer searches for a product
- a customer browses through a category of products
- a customer purchases an item
- a customer has a problem and wishes to contact support
- a customer wants to know whether you'll ship to their country
- a new user registers an account on the site

During the development of your site, these use cases can guide you (as well as your web designers and developers) while working on the design.

Conducting a Test

Usability testing is as easy as sitting down with people, giving them some tasks to complete, and watching how they go about it. If you're observant and keep your eyes and ears open while they do this, you'll be able to see where they find it easy or hard to move through your site.

As a general rule, try to have at least six users complete your testing tasks for you. If you're making improvements to an existing site, then your users would ideally

---

[1] http://useit.com/alertbox/20000319.html

be a mix of existing customers with some familiarity with your web site and products, and users with no knowledge of your web site at all. Of course, if your site is new, they'll all be unaccustomed to it.

When you're observing a test, be on the lookout for situations where the user expresses frustration or concern with the task, wanders completely off the path you expected them to take, or feels the need to ask questions. These are your clues that the interface is in some way lacking and needs your attention.

There's software to help record your user tests for later viewing—for Windows, try Morae,[2] and for the Mac, try Silverback.[3] Each application allows you to record users' expressions and opinions while capturing screen activity. Meanwhile, if you're having difficulty finding users in the real world who are willing to sit down with you and look at your site, try FeedbackArmy[4]: you provide the URL and a set of questions, and Feedback Army sources people to take a look.

Usability testing is a broad topic, and there's plenty more to learn. You'll find a great introduction to usability testing in an article from *24 Ways*, called Fast and Simple Usability Testing.[5]

Testing Early with Mockups and Prototypes

It's a great idea to test your site early, before your design has even been coded, to help guide the development process. For example, design mockups can be printed and used for simpler tests, in which a user could point to the parts of the screen they might use. You can even build small functional prototypes using Flash, PowerPoint, or even good old HTML that replicate the intended behavior of your system. To learn more about this technique, check out this article from The Hiser Group.[6]

---

[2] http://techsmith.com/morae.asp

[3] http://silverbackapp.com/

[4] http://feedbackarmy.com/

[5] http://24ways.org/2006/fast-and-simple-usability-testing

[6] http://hiser.com.au/articles/dtech_paper_mock-ups.html/section/483

Interpreting and Acting

When you have some results from your usability tests, it's time to act on them. If your tests show that users fail to meet a goal, or stumble on certain tasks, you'll need to re-evaluate your design and solve the problem. Discuss the results with your design and development team, and ask them to rework parts of the design that could help.

Once you've implemented solutions for a specific usability problem, ensure that you test it again. While you might have solved one troublesome issue, the solution might reveal new, previously unseen problems further along in the process.

Employing Usability Experts

If your budget permits, you may wish to employ the services of a usability consultant. Quality usability professionals can cost a bit, however they can have a substantial impact on the commercial success of your web site. Like any consultant, experience counts. Check their references, and look for demonstrated positive outcomes for other clients. Find the right person and they'll bring best-practice usability techniques to your design, as well as ensure efficient and effective testing and measurement.

If you're considering hiring a usability expert, I'd suggest you engage them early in the design process, as that's when they'll do their best work. They can also point you in the right direction before there's a major stuff up—it's much more difficult, and more expensive, to fix things at the last minute.

Accessibility

One of the most beautiful things about the Web is that it breaks down so many communication barriers. It eliminates geographical boundaries, social or ethnic differences, and even limitations such as cognitive or physiological disabilities. It's one of the reasons to love the Web; if you're doing business online, you can have a long-term relationship with a wheelchair-bound blind customer just as easily as you can an able-bodied person.

Back in the good ol' days of the Web, when pages were just simple text and a small amount of graphics, it was easy to ensure that your web site was accessible to all comers. As modern web sites have become more complex, so have the challenges of ensuring your web site is accessible—but in all honesty, it's quite manageable. Yes, there are a few extra tasks to do which may add some additional cost and time; however, it will be a small fraction of the overall design of your site. What's more, if you work on these challenges early rather than trying to "bolt on" a solution later, the process will be a lot smoother.

Why care about accessibility?

Your social conscience should be motive enough to ensure your web site is accessible to all. However, if you require more motivation, it's as simple as this. First, it's simply good business sense to make sure all your customers are able to perform actions or make purchases on your web site. Second, in many jurisdictions it's illegal to discriminate against people with a disability, and you could leave yourself open to legal action if you ignore the requirements.

Discrimination Lawsuits Cost You Big Money

In most places it's a legal requirement that a public place—such as a store, a railway station, or a sporting venue—must provide facilities for people with a disability or other impairment, for example, rails, ramps, or Braille signage. For the exact same reasons, you need to be able to accommodate people with a disability when you provide an online service. If you fail do so, even if it's just an oversight, the law in your area might consider that you've committed an act of discrimination.

Here's a recent, real-world example. In 2006, the National Federation of the Blind filed a class action against retail giant, Target. The case was based on the premise that target.com[7] was inaccessible to visually impaired individuals and that Target had refused to take steps to rectify the situation. After a two-year legal battle, Target settled the case, paying $US6 million to a fund set up for individuals affected by the inaccessibility of the site.[8] $US6 million for a company the size of Target is little more than a slap on the wrist, but it does set a precedent, and provides a stern warning as to why you need to ensure your web site meets acceptable accessibility standards. Make sure that you're aware of the discrimination laws in your area and act accordingly within any guidelines.

---

[7] http://target.com/
[8] http://nfbtargetlawsuit.com/

How to Check Your Web Site's Accessibility

If you're hiring a web development company to create your web site for you, your brief needs to include accessibility. A good developer should already include this as part of their services, but it's important to specify this explicitly in the project so that you know what you're getting. For more information on the varying types of accessibility issues to be considered, visit the W3C guidelines on accessibility.[9] Even with an agreement in place, it's important to make tests of your own to ensure your site is accessible and complies with any relevant laws.

There are several guidelines and techniques for accessible web sites published by the W3C, which you'll find on their Web Accessibility Initiative web site.[10] The techniques include ways to build and test your site, and it's important that your developers are familiar with what they suggest. To start with, here are five quick tests for your site:

1. Validate your HTML and CSS. Assistive technology—appliances or software that can assist a disabled user—work best with valid markup. There are two easy ways to check whether your site does this correctly. One is to install browser plugins or add-ons to help, such as the validation add-on for Firefox,[11] and another is to use the W3C's online validator.[12] The validator will tell you about any markup errors in your site.

2. View your web site using a screen reader. A screen reader is a piece of software that reads out the contents of your site using synthesized speech, and is designed to assist people who have difficulties reading from a screen. A common screen reader is Freedom Scientific's JAWS.[13] A license for JAWS is quite expensive, though you can use it for free for a maximum of half an hour at a time. The Fangs add-on for Firefox can show you the text that would be read by JAWS, which is an inexpensive and easy alternative. Alternatively, try using the text-only browser,

---

[9] http://www.w3.org/TR/WCAG20/

[10] http://w3.org/WAI/guid-tech.html

[11] https://addons.mozilla.org/en-US/firefox/addon/249

[12] http://validator.w3.org/

[13] http://freedomscientific.com/products/fs/jaws-product-page.asp

Lynx.[14] A text-only browser is quite different to a screen reader, but many of the same issues that face screen reader users will become evident in this browser.

3. View your web site using magnification software—a tool that zooms in on a portion of your screen. Use Magnifier if you're using Windows, and the Universal Access panel for a Mac. Both are bundled with the operating system and are explained in the help.

4. Navigate your web site without using your mouse. Some people have difficulties with using a mouse. Instead, they may use keyboards alone, or alternative pointing devices such as a joystick to navigate around their computer. To try this out for yourself, open your favorite web browser and try navigating using only your keyboard.

5. Think about the language you're using. The text on your web site should be natural, reasonably easy to read, and use as little jargon as possible. Remember, you could be dealing with people with limited English skills. And in the case of people with English as a second language, it becomes an accessibility issue. You can gain an idea of how easy it is to read your site by using the Readability Test Tool at Juicy Studio, which uses a number of reading ease tests to assess the content of your site.[15]

If you can navigate and use your site with these methods, and your site validates, then you can be confident your web site is that much closer to being accessible. You may wish to take your tests a step further and ensure that individuals with disabilities are included with your user testing, providing a more definitive answer. This may be difficult to achieve and could require that you hire a specialist usability consultant. Many usability consultancies have experience with accessibility testing.

Performance and Scalability

A slow web site is just like a slow freeway—your visitors will become impatient and frustrated while waiting for conditions to speed up. Worse yet, they'll often click the back button on their browser and veer elsewhere to make a purchase.

---

[14] http://vordweb.co.uk/standards/download_lynx.htm
[15] http://juicystudio.com/services/readability.php

In Andrew B. King's book *Website Optimization*,[16] Google has claimed that a 500 millisecond increase in page load times decreased traffic and advertising revenue by 20%. Amazon has reported that for every 100 millisecond increase in load times, conversion rates decrease by 1%. If two of the biggest and most recognized web sites can lose revenue when their performance decreases, chances are you will too.

Scalability

When you're viewing your web site before it launches, there's little or no other traffic—the only people seeing it are you and your team, so it's likely to be very responsive with plenty of extra capacity for traffic. Then you put your web site out there in the real world, and things change. If you're doing a great job with marketing, your visitor numbers will start to grow—and so will your page load times. On top of that, if your web site gains prominence on a social networking site like Digg[17] or Reddit,[18] you could suddenly receive more than a week's worth of traffic in one day. How will your servers handle that?

Planning your system's capacity is usually the responsibility of your hosting service or system administrator. Still, it's important to know what your limits are and what capacity you have for growth on short notice. Talk to your server administration team about high traffic situations—ask them about contingency plans in the event of an unexpected spike in traffic. Every minute your site is unavailable, you're losing money!

Battle of the Browsers

If you're from a traditional marketing background, one of the biggest differences you'll find in online marketing is how little control you have over the way your web site and advertising creative is presented to visitors. When you're creating advertising for a magazine, for example, it's easy to maintain complete consistency in height, width, and color. The challenge with online marketing is that all those variables can alter from visitor to visitor, depending on their browser, their operating system, even the device they're using. This unpredictable presentation creates additional challenges that you need to be aware of.

---

[16] Sebastopol: O'Reilly, 2008
[17] http://digg.com/
[18] http://reddit.com/

Screen Resolutions and Monitor Sizes

The size of the screen that a visitor uses to view your web site can range from tiny portable devices, like phones, to 50-inch monitors, and everything in between. As well as screen sizes varying, the available space in the window can differ too. Your visitors might have a maximized window, or one that only covers half of the monitor. Because it's hard to predict the size of a user's window, your site should be usable when viewed on a range of screen sizes.

Varying Browsers and Versions

While Internet Explorer is still the most popular web browser, other browsers are gaining market share at a rapid pace. Browsers such as Firefox, Google Chrome, Opera, and Safari make up the bulk of the competition, however there are still many more around. Each browser has its own unique method of rendering a web page, so if you view your web site through Firefox, chances are it might look slightly different to its appearance in Safari or Internet Explorer.

And on top of that, there are also different versions of each web browser, each with its own quirks and problems. It's unlikely that all of your readers will have taken the time to upgrade to the latest version of their browser of choice, and each one ought to be catered for.

Test Your Site

The quickest way to run a test on your web site is to download the five most used browsers—Internet Explorer, Firefox, Safari, Opera, and Google Chrome—and view your web site with each. You'll either see a web site that is cross-browser compatible, or you'll discover that in certain browsers your web site is completely unusable. If you're pressed for time or unable to install numerous browser versions, there are services on the Web that will make screenshots for you. One good, affordable example is Browsercam.[19]

As with accessibility, it's important that cross-browser compatibility and a flexible layout form part of your web site design planning. And remember—a site working perfectly on your screen is no guarantee it will do so on others.

---

[19] http://browsercam.com/

Your Homepage

Your homepage is like the front door to your business. While some of your traffic will enter your web site through a *side door*, such as a product listing or a blog post, for the most part your homepage will act as a funnel for your traffic. Homepage design is so important that world-renowned usability expert, Jakob Nielsen published an entire book dedicated to homepage design.[20] A well-planned and designed homepage should achieve a number of goals, which we'll explore in detail.

Clearly Explain Who You Are

If you were to introduce yourself to a sales prospect in person, you need to be clear and succinct: you'd tell them who you are, what you do, and how your product can help them. Equally, your site's purpose should be immediately obvious from visiting the homepage. First-time users should be able to gain an instant understanding of what your web site is about, and what they can do here. If they have to spend more than a few seconds puzzling it out, they'll hit the back button and take their money elsewhere. Use a tag line or summary text near the top of the page so that it's easy to find, and make sure that there are clear pathways to the major functions of your site.

Include a Search

Web sites are growing larger and more complicated, and users are more comfortable than ever using search tools to find what they're looking for, so including a search bar on your site is important. A poor performing search can create additional frustration, so be sure to choose a search tool that works well. A good search engine goes beyond just finding pages—it finds the *best* pages. If your search fails to deliver the best results, your users will go to another site that can bring them what they want.

Provide Fresh Web Site Content

Show your users that this is an active site that is updated and cared for, rather than a one-time project. If you publish articles, blogs, or newsletters, make sure this is

---

[20] Nielsen, Jakob and Tahir, Marie: *Homepage Usability: 50 Websites Deconstructed* (Indianapolis: New Riders Press, 2001)

reflected somehow on your homepage. You also may want to consider running feeds from social networking sites, such as mentions of your business on Twitter.[21]

Keep Your Corporate Information Together

Corporate information such as policies, business/investor information, contact details, and the like are important pages of information to have on your web site—however, they're usually considered less important to your actual web site users. You should keep all this supplementary information grouped and away from your main functions. The footer of SitePoint[22] is a good example of this—it contains links to pages about the company, a contact page, and other details.

Design that Enhances

Good design is as much about problem solving as it is about great aesthetics. A good design should enhance a visitor's experience with your site, and the same needs to occur with your homepage. Your usability testing will provide insight into user challenges and a good designer will embrace these challenges and work the design so it solves these problems. When you're planning a design, start with a user's needs and solve any dilemmas with the design.

Lovely Landing Pages

Landing pages are your money pages. They're one of the strongest tools you have to convert visitors into customers. Much of your marketing activity will be geared around attracting visitors to these pages, so the way you construct these will have a significant impact on your income.

The difference between a lackluster landing page and a great one can be summed up in just a few basic principles. Let's take a look.

Focus on One Objective

A landing page should focus on one primary objective—a call to action. Your call to action might be to encourage a visitor to order a specific product, sign up for a newsletter, or create a new user account on your site. You should ensure that

---

[21] http://twitter.com/
[22] http://sitepoint.com/

everything on your landing page is focused on encouraging that objective to be met—images, text, even the layout should help encourage the user to act.

Your visitor should find it easy to understand what it is that you want them to do. Your call to action should appear at the top, middle, and end of your landing page and should be clear and concise.

Out of the Way!

The easier you can make a process, the more conversions you'll make. Asking your customers to jump through hoops to answer your call to action will only push them away.

If there's only one part of your site that's tested for usability, your transaction process should be it. Step through the entire process and eliminate any sticking points you observe. For example, a customer clicks an Order Now button on an advertisement for a product, but instead is taken to a landing page. You should simply take them directly to your checkout with the product already in the cart. They've already clicked Order Now—so move out of the way, and let them do it as easily as possible.

Use Visuals to Drive Focus

The use of imagery on your landing page should serve to drive focus on your objective. You can use illustrations to provide visual insight into a product as well as aid the explanation of a process. Your visitors, just like you, are busy people with limited time and attention. If your visuals are distracting or vague, you'll test their concentration and patience.

Above the Fold

The fold is an imaginary line that delineates the part of a web page that can be seen without scrolling. As we learned earlier in this chapter, there is so much variation in screen sizes that it's basically impossible to know where the fold is. Web site analytics packages—facilities that collect statistics about your users—can tell you about your most popular screen resolutions, allowing for a guesstimate. Having said that, as a rule of thumb, you should ensure that your most important sales message appears close to the top of your landing page.

Page Layout

Some of the most effective landing pages feature a single column of text, and are very simple in design. If you're introducing two or even three columns in your landing page, you need to ensure that all the surrounding content supports your primary objective. This might include things like customer reviews, secure payment processing information, or any added incentives to buy.

What's your value proposition?

Your **value proposition**—the way you describe what the customer can expect to gain from their purchase—should be crystal clear. The clearer your value proposition, the *stickier* your landing page will be; the stickier your page, the more sales you'll make. But if the benefits of your product or service are unclear, a visitor will go to another place for what they need.

Building Customer Confidence

We've all heard stories of disappointing online purchases, bad customer service experiences, and even scams. All new visitors arrive at a site with an initial level of concern or caution about the risk—no matter how small—of dealing with you for the first time. You can reassure your visitors by including page elements that convey trustworthiness. Use credibility indicators such as awards, privacy policies, certifications, and testimonials to foster trust, and include statements that attest to our longevity, such as "Serving the needs of Chicago for more than 15 years." To alleviate a reader's reservations about the quality of your product, show off your positive customer reviews and industry awards, and use money-back guarantees. A happy, confident visitor is much more likely to become a customer.

Testing Conversions

Landing page optimization can be very scientific, and a common theme of all landing page experts is to test everything. There are two main types of testing: A/B testing, and multivariate. Let's explore both.

A/B testing

A/B testing is the term used to describe a simple test of two versions of your landing page—version A and version B. You serve these two different web pages randomly to your visitors to identify which converts at the highest rate. A/B testing is very focused and precise. It allows you to test even the smallest adjustment to a landing page and give a definitive response. It's the slowest form of testing, but the most accurate.

Multivariate Testing

Multivariate testing is a little more complex. With an A/B test you might run a long copy versus short copy approach; with a multivariate test, you run more than two scenarios.

A multivariate test allows you to test any or all of the possible combinations, with the results showing you which combinations worked best. For example, you may wish to test long versus short text, one column versus two, and two different order buttons—all at the same time. The results of a multivariate test for these might look like this:

Test	Conversion
Long Copy / One column / Blue button	0.78%
Long Copy / One column / Red button	1.1%
Long Copy / Two column / Blue button	0.4%
Long Copy / Two column / Red button	0.2%
Short Copy / One column / Blue button	1.2%
Short Copy / One column / Red button	2.3%
Short Copy / Two column / Blue button	1.7%
Short Copy / Two column / Red button	1.5%

This test would indicate that short copy generally performed better than long copy, and one column with a red button outperformed them all.

Usually, you'll need to run a multivariate test for some time in order to gain a large sample size. Multivariate testing is great for identifying overall approaches to your web site, however it lacks the precision of an A/B test.

An Evolving Entity

Your homepage, your landing pages, and all the other pages in your web site should never remain stagnant. It's most unlikely that the design for your web site will be ready to go *out of the box*. Your visitors' behavior is impossible to completely predict, even with an extensive testing plan, so you need to be prepared for ongoing changes to your site. There could be small tweaks to pages to increase conversion rates, or larger, fundamental changes if your current design is creating too many challenges for your visitors. Even if your site works fine, you might simply want to improve it even more.

The needs and motivation of your visitors will also change over time—so your web site needs to evolve along with them. You should continually test, analyze, and refine your web site to improve conversions and keep a step ahead of your competitors.

We've covered quite a broad range of topics in this chapter—let's turn these concepts into a quick checklist for your own web site:

1. Is your web site accessible?
2. How usable is your web site?
3. Does your design solve problems rather than create them?
4. Is your web site cross-browser compatible?
5. Are your page load times as fast as they can be?
6. Can your web site deal with increased demand?
7. Is your homepage the shining light of your web site?
8. Are your landing pages geared for maximum conversion?
9. Are you ready for ongoing testing?

If you can answer yes to all of these questions, congratulations! You're well on your way to a high-conversion web site.

Search Engine Optimization

Own or run a web site and you'll be approached by organizations or individuals offering search engine marketing services. **Search engine marketing** is any kind of activity that's intended to bring traffic from a search engine to another web site. A common source of confusion when discussing search engines occurs within its two main disciplines: search engine optimization, and search engine advertising. While both relate specifically to search engine applications, their techniques and goals are quite different.

Search engine optimization (SEO) is the function of improving a web site's position in the results of a search engine query for a target set of keywords. This includes optimizing your own pages—making your site attractive to search engines, as well as encouraging other sites to link back to you.

Search engine advertising is when advertisements are displayed to search engine visitors when a defined set of search terms is requested. For the most part, these advertising campaigns are based on a Pay Per Click model where you pay a set amount each time your ad is clicked on.

Search engine advertising is covered in detail in Chapter 8. In this chapter, we'll concentrate on search engine optimization, and how you can use it to cause explosive growth in your site's traffic.

Understanding Search Engines

A **search engine** is the main starting point for most people attempting to find products, services, or information on the Web. Just think how many times you've used Google, Yahoo, or MSN to find an item yourself when unsure of where else to start. Since about 1993, demand for search engines has exploded.[1] To ignore search engines as a part of your marketing mix is like forgetting to zip up your fly when you dress in the morning—you just end up looking silly.

The Role of a Search Engine

Search engines have played one of the biggest roles in the growth of the Internet. The sole purpose of a Web search engine is to help find the most relevant web sites for a user. When a user enters a search term or a phrase into a search engine, the search engine examines its database of known web sites, decides what's most relevant, and returns the results to the user. When you consider that there are billions of web sites in existence, search engines allow us to find that needle in the giant haystack that is the Web.

Search Engine Results Pages

Search for "SEO" in Google, and you'll receive over 267 million results. As I mentioned earlier, part of the search engine's job is to list all the records it finds, ranked in order of what is most to least relevant, grouped into pages. We call these **Search Engine Results Pages**—or simply SERPs. Your objective in search engine marketing is to increase your site's ranking on the SERPS for keywords that are important to your business—preferably making it to the first page, and ideally nailing the top spot. Needless to say, the distance you end up from first place can make a huge difference to the amount of traffic you gain from search engines—let alone being the 267 millionth!

---

[1] http://groups.google.com/group/comp.infosystems.www/msg/4b58ee36a52f21ee

A study by Microsoft shows some fairly typical click-through rates on results found on the first SERP.[2]

Front Page Position	Click Through Percentage
1st	89%
2nd	33%
4th	17%
5th	17%
7th	6%

As you can see, there's an enormous difference just between first place and second—and the percentage of people who click through gets even smaller still, until you see just 6% clicking on the result in seventh place.

How Search Engines Collect Information

Search engines build and maintain their massive database by sending out millions of small applications into deep, dark depths of the Internet every day. Called **spiders**, these little applications play an important role in how your site will perform in search engines. Spiders continuously crawl through web sites, collating information and updating the search engines' database of sites. If a spider has problems viewing, interpreting, or navigating your site, you'll struggle to perform well in engine results. Later in this chapter, we'll go into more detail on how to ensure your site is spider-friendly.

How a Search Engine Determines Rank

Exactly how a Search Engine application determines rank is one of the most closely guarded secrets of the web industry. In the early days, companies like Google would openly discuss the algorithm they used.[3] Nowadays, with so much more money at stake, it's smarter for an online search engine provider to keep private the most important aspect of their business. A competitor might replicate the algorithm, or any weaknesses in the algorithm may be exploited.

---

[2] ftp://ftp.research.microsoft.com/pub/tr/TR-2007-01.pdf
[3] http://buzzle.com/editorials/6-10-2005-71368.asp

©RankedHard.com - Created by BigOakInc.com / Art by Kelly Ishikawa - KellyIshikawa.com

Figure 4.1. The dark art of SEO[4]

This means search engine marketing has become more of an art than a science—in fact, in the industry, it's quite common to joke that it could even be something of a mysterious, black art, as the comic in Figure 4.1 suggests. Why? Because only a handful of people know exactly how Google really ranks one site over another—and that's because they work for Google. The same goes for all the other major search engines. Extremely tenacious and smart individuals have conducted months upon months of research to develop hypotheses on how search engines work—but it'll never be a matter of absolute fact.

---

[4] Used with permission of Big Oak SEO: http://bigoakinc.com

Another important point to remember is that search engines are continually evolving applications. In 2008 alone, it was reported that the algorithm Google uses to rank sites changed over 400 times! So if search engine optimization is a part of your marketing strategy—and it should be—it's essential that you involve yourself in the SEO community to keep abreast of changes as they come to hand. We'll talk about some of these communities and key sources of information later in this chapter.

The Big Three

Right now, Google dominates the search engine market. If you want the greatest return on your investment then you'll need to focus the bulk of your time on Google. But there are two main competitors to Google, Yahoo and MSN, which also need to be considered.

Outside of the big three, there are many smaller search engines—but these are only worth your time targeting if they're specifically focused on your niche.

Still, it's important to involve yourself in the search engine community so that you can stay informed of new search engines as they arrive. Who knows, one day there might be a search engine to rival Google, and if you're one of the first to establish a presence, you could find yourself in a position money can't buy!

So focus on the big three, seek out search engines specific to your niche, and keep an eye on upcoming engines to ensure you have a search engine optimization strategy that's geared for maximum return on investment.

The Different Hats of SEO

Once you become involved in Search Engine Optimization, you're going to eventually see discussions about the color of one's hat: is it black, or white?

There are two main approaches to search engine optimization—**white hat** techniques are those based on common sense and fair play, while **black hat** techniques are based on shady tactics and spam.

Black hat SEO marketers are about achieving results as fast as possible, generating as much cash as they can before search engines ban their sites. They'll employ taboo tactics such as:

- **cloaking**—a technique of showing different content than what a user sees to a search engine in order to receive more favorable—but undeserving—search hits
- **hidden links**—links on a page that are invisible to a user, but quite visible to a search engine
- useless commenting on blogs, just to include a URL (this is especially common behavior among young black hat SEO marketers)

When search engines detect black hat techniques in use, the site will often be removed entirely from the search engine's index. If you're serious about SEO, stay away from black hat techniques.

White hat marketers employ a common sense, ethical approach to SEO. These techniques include:

- creating quality content
- building legitimate links
- developing a solid keyword strategy
- maximizing spider friendliness
- building page rank over time

Although white hat SEO might lack instant results, the lasting success is worth the wait.

Creating Your Own SEO Strategy

You now should have an understanding of the basic principles of a search engine; now it's time to look at some specific strategies to grow your own search engine traffic. I've broken these strategies into three main concepts: keywords, web site design, and site popularity. A good SEO strategy will encompass all three elements. Let's explore all of them.

Keywords

Keywords are the foundation of your search engine optimization strategy. Unfortunately, detailed keyword research is too often forgotten or poorly implemented, sending a search engine optimization campaign crashing to the ground.

So what are keywords? They can be a single word, several words, or a phrase that potential customers will enter into a search engine that is applicable to the products/service you provide. The beauty of a search engine is that you're able to target very generic keywords or search terms, or drill down to more specific phrases.

Identify Generic Keywords

Generic search terms are the most basic terms used to describe a topic. Identifying the generic terms for the type of traffic you'd like on your site is the first step in your keyword strategy. These generic terms will always be the most frequently used in search engines, while subsequent, more specific phrases usually have a considerable drop-off. But beware of deluding yourself into thinking you can grab the top spot for a generic term. It's almost impossible, and requires a massive investment in time and money.

Even if you do manage to achieve top billing on a generic term, you'll need to find ways to return your significant investment—and this could be more complicated than you think. Let's say you run a company that sells horse blankets, and you've somehow managed to rank top spot for the term "horse." Granted, the site would receive a lot of search engine traffic, but would that traffic be worthwhile? Sure, there would be some potential customers, but you'd also attract visitors who would never be interested in buying a horse blanket; instead, they might be looking for information on horse racing, or horse art, or even rocking horses. While grabbing a top spot on a generic term might be good for traffic, you might be unable to convert all that into solid business.

So why identify them? Your list of generic search terms are your starting point, allowing you to drill down into more specific phrases for the products or services you provide. Jot down the most generic terms applicable. In most cases these will be single words, but in some instances—for example, real estate—two would be applicable.

Having identified your top-level keywords, we can now move on to the next step: choosing more focused terms.

Add More Focused Terms

This is where the fun really starts—with your list of generic terms, it's now time to identify the more specific keywords that your SEO campaign should target; these focused terms usually consist of two to three words. In order to identify the ideal set of terms, we need to consider a number of factors, such as overall search volume, competitiveness of the search term, and variations. Your end result will be a long list of potential search terms to target.

Phrases and Modifiers

Phrases are additional product/service specific terms that appear alongside a generic term in a search engine. Horse Blankets, Horse Floats, Horse Shoes, are examples of possible secondary search terms with our horse example that form phrases. Modifiers are also important, as they are more common terms used in a related search. Cheap Horse Products or Horses for Sale are examples of introducing common terms to modify your search phrases. By introducing common terms you can influence the type of traffic you'll generate on your site.

Singular and Plural

Search engines are sometimes unable to determine the similarity between the plural and singular form of a word. While they are becoming smarter, there are still some discrepancies: for example, there are significantly more results in Google for "horse blankets" (over 2.5 million) than the singular version (just 573,000). Depending on your search terms, however, the plural version may actually be a more searched-for term than the singular form, so be sure to include both forms on your keyword list.

Use Variations and Misspellings

There's often more than one way to describe your keyword, and variations can be a nifty way to unearth opportunities. Search engines like Google will often suggest changes for misspellings or variations; however there's still some room to optimize for different variations. For example, some people might be searching for a "horse rug" rather than a "horse blanket," or perhaps a reader looking to take a trip overseas is planning to take a "holiday" rather than a "vacation."

Variations such as changing verbs to nouns can also be a way to catch clicks. For example, you might find that some people use the search phrase, "horseback ride" rather than "horseback riding."

Watch Out for Common Words

There are so many instances of common words (for example: a, of, the), it would be pointless for search engines to record their occurrence. Most search engines have a large list of common words which they ignore in their index. These are known as stop words, or noise words. However, these excluded terms are not always obvious, and longer common words may be included such as 'promotion'. Just to add some complexity, the list differs for all search engines.

It's still okay to include these common words if they're relevant, as some terms take on a different meaning when they're contained within certain phrases. For example, "welcome" is often excluded since it's used frequently on many sites ("Welcome to Widgets, Inc."), but if you're searching for a "Welcome Inn Hotel," the word takes on more relevance.

Identifying Your Ideal Keywords

There's a growing number of tools to assist you with identifying search terms. Google has its own keyword tool, which is free and easy to use.[5] Just enter a generic term, press a button, and you'll receive a long list of variations. You can sort that list based on relevance, average search volume, last month's search volume, and advertiser competition; there's even the option to export it as a spreadsheet for later use.

From this list, you can filter out irrelevant keywords and conduct further searches based on the shortlist. Using the Google Keyword Tool should help you uncover many options, and once you apply some of the variations above, such as plurals and misspellings, your keyword list should look quite healthy.

While these tools are extremely helpful, you should look to other sources of information—such as your competition—for ideas. This can be as simple as looking for words on their web site that have a high density—that is, they appear frequently.

---

[5] https://adwords.google.com/select/KeywordToolExternal

It's also helpful to observe the kinds of words and phrases people use to describe your products and services on community forums, or on applications like Twitter and Facebook. You might go as far as running a small user test—for example, asking people to search for horse equipment—and observe the keywords they enter.

Localization

If you're providing a physical service, you may be limited by geographical boundaries, so your keywords should reflect this. You might choose to use keywords for a city, state, or country, but make sure you include abbreviations or variations in your keyword list—for example, BC as well as British Columbia.

Using Brand Names

Using brand names is an alternative to descriptive keyword targeting. You might be a retailer selling brand name goods, so ranking well on a particular brand name search can be highly beneficial. Targeting another company's trademark may cause problems though—so it's a good idea to check with your legal counsel before implementing this.

Deciding Which Terms to Target

By now you should have a long list of potential keywords to target, so it's time to collate the information that will help you trim this to a much smaller list. In order to achieve this, we'll need to collate some statistics on each of our potential keywords.

First, we need to determine the search volume for a particular phrase. Again, Google's Keyword Tool is ideal for obtaining this information; there's a column to indicate the search volumes—the average and the previous month's. Record this against all your potential keywords.

Next, we need to determine the level of competition for the keywords, in order for us to judge the effort required to dominate that particular term. We can do this in three ways: by advertiser demand, current top performers, and link text.

Determining Advertiser Demand

The first step is to collate the advertiser demand for the keyword. This shows the volume of advertisers wanting to use the Sponsored Links section of a search engine for advertising. If there's a lot of competition among advertisers here, then it's a safe bet that there's significant search traffic.

As I mentioned earlier, this is available through Google's free Keyword Tool and should be recorded against each potential keyword.

Identifying Current Top Performers

The second form of enquiry is a little more time-consuming. You need to analyze sites that currently appear on the first page of your target keyword. This is where a new metric comes into play: the overall popularity and authority of the web site. In Google, this is called PageRank.

Google guards its PageRank algorithm very closely, so I'm unable to give you a definitive answer on how a page's PageRank is actually calculated. One aspect we're sure of though, is that incoming links play a vital role.

A PageRank is a number between 0 and 10. Sites that rank 4 or less are relatively easy to surpass, while sites ranking 5 and above require a much more concentrated campaign.

To determine your competition's PageRank, search with each of your target keywords, and identify the top ranked sites. Use a PageRank checking tool to obtain the PageRank for each of the top ranking sites (those that appear on the first page of the search results) for each of your potential keywords.

Currently, no one tool can accurately determine PageRank. Google's toolbar[6] contains a PageRank indicator, but even this can be inaccurate. Google updates PageRank frequently, but the information displayed in the Google toolbar is only updated approximately every three months.

---

[6] http://toolbar.google.com/

Link Text

Links play an important role in reinforcing the relevance of a web site to a search engine. If a site has many incoming links, then it can be safely assumed that the site is popular; additionally, the text used for the links adds further context to help a search engine determine the topic of the web page on the other end of that link.

To determine the number of links with your keywords in the text, search in Google for "inanchor:your keywords." This will show you the overall number of links that contain this keyword. For keyword phrases, it's wise to also determine the results for each individual word as well as the entire phrase.

Relevance

Now that we've dealt with the strategies for maximizing your search engine traffic, the final piece of information required to complete your keyword analysis is the relevance of your site to your potential keyword or phrase. It's useful to think about relevance in terms of the number of people who would have used that search term, then arrived at your site, then felt that it was relevant to them. Of course, it's hard to be sure about how people feel about the relevance of your site, since we're unable to read the minds of every single person who entered the search term—but we can have a good guess.

To do this we can use a keyword analysis tool like WordTracker.[7] Using the application, search for one of your keywords. WordTracker reveals a list of related searches and their volume—grab the ones that contain your phrase, and enter them and their volumes into a spreadsheet. Add up each of the volumes to obtain a total figure. Then, for each of the phrases that are actually relevant to your site, calculate the volumes of each as a percentage of the total.

From this, you should gain an indication of how many people—of those who are using your original phrase as part of their search—will find your site relevant.

Let's try an example. In Table 4.1, we can see a keyword relevance analysis for a site that lists show jumping and dressage horses for sale. We've started out with the phrase "horses for sale" and received a number of phrases, including those words.

---

[7] http://wordtracker.com/

Many of the phrases are about workhorses or thoroughbreds, so we can exclude those and concentrate on those phrases that relate specifically to show horses.

Table 4.1. Relevance analysis for "horses for sale"

Keywords	Approximate average search volume	% total volume (relevant phrases only)
andalusian horses for sale	1600	
arab horses for sale	320	
arabian horses for sale	6600	
auction horses for sale	58	
draft horses for sale	5400	
dressage horses for sale	5400	7.13%
event horses for sale	1000	1.32%
gelding horses for sale	590	0.78%
horses for sale or lease	480	0.63%
jumping horses for sale	1900	2.51%
miniature horses for sale	8100	
paint horses for sale	14800	
performance horses for sale	390	0.51%
quarter horses for sale	18100	
ranch horses for sale	2900	
reining horses for sale	3600	
riding horses for sale	1300	1.72%
sport horses for sale	1300	1.72%
thoroughbred horses for sale	1900	
Totals	75738	16.32%

If the total is quite small, this may be the wrong keyword or phrase to target. If it's high, then you can be more certain your site will be relevant to a searcher. In our above example, a relevance of only a little over 16% should probably remain low on the list of priorities.

Return on Investment

By now, you should have a strong list of phrases with supporting statistics on how often they are searched for, how much competition exists for the particular term/s, and how relevant your site is to those phrases. You now need to determine which terms will give you the greatest return on your investment.

The keywords you should choose will largely depend on your specific circumstances. You might wish to target a competitive keyword that delivers 10,000 new visitors per week but requires huge effort; alternately, you might wish to start small and target an infrequently used search term with little or no competition, which requires less effort. Figure 4.2 shows the relationship between competition, search volume, and effort.

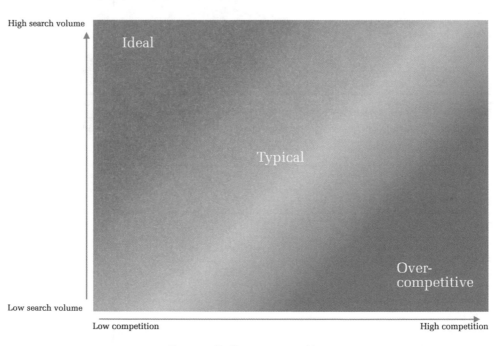

Figure 4.2. Traffic versus competition

Naturally, you should be targeting the search terms that will give you the most relevant traffic for your effort. Look for the variations on your keywords that have search volumes acceptable to you—preferably those with high relevance and low competition.

Once you've decided on your target keywords, it's time to start the next phase of your search engine campaign: working on your site design and content.

Site Design

There are many factors to consider when designing a web site, with search engine optimization being just one of several. It might seem as though designers and copywriters' creative efforts are at odds with SEO but, in truth, beautiful design and meaningful text can exist harmoniously with effective search engine optimization. A good designer with an understanding of SEO concepts should be able to solve any design problem without negatively impacting SEO. As part of their role, designers are already considering different kinds of users, multiple web browsers, and a range of screen sizes; copywriters, too, work hard to make sure that the content of your site is the best it can be to all types of users. Adding just one more user—a search engine spider—is barely stretching them.

Page Design Elements

Understanding the elements that are important to SEO is a task independent to knowing how to design a web site. Still, there are some principles you need a good comprehension of in order to have an intelligent conversation with your web developer.

The code that contains the content of a web site is called HTML. Text, images, or other media are contained with HTML elements, and these elements define the *meaning* of the content. The most important elements from an SEO perspective are the heading, paragraph, title, hyperlinks, and meta elements.

Heading Elements

Heading elements are exactly what they sound like—headings for your web page. They range from H1 to H6, with H1 being the most important heading. Your page should contain one H1 heading and ideally, that heading should include your keywords. A search engine spider will look at headings to determine relevance for your site. Subsequent headings should use the secondary heading elements in order of importance, and where possible include your keywords. Take care to expand on your keywords to form proper headings so that they make sense. Real visitors need to be engaged by meaningful headings so that they feel compelled to read the rest of the page.

Paragraphs

Most of the text on your page will be contained in paragraph elements. You should endeavor to include your keywords in the first few paragraphs, but not at the expense of the text's meaning. Your copy should flow naturally and be easy to read. Focus on your communication foremost, and then bring in your keywords.

Some SEO experts suggest that it's a poor idea for your text to be keyword dense, and that search engines may even interpret this as **keyword stuffing**—a shady tactic used by black hats, in which irrelevant keywords are overused in the content specifically to trick spiders. Yet what that threshold actually is is a bit of mystery, let alone other factors that might come into play. Just make sure your text is flowing and natural, and you'll be okay.

Page Title

The page title is important for a good search result ranking, as well as the huge difference it can make to click-throughs from search engine results pages. What is contained in your title tag is what will be presented in the search engine results page as the heading for the result. As the example below shows, the more detail, the better. You should ensure that your keywords appear in the first ten words of your title.

Poor   Horse Blankets

Better   Quality Horse Blankets

Best   Premium Quality Horse Blankets—Lowest Prices Guaranteed

Hyperlinks

You've already learned about anchor text in the keyword research section of this chapter, but links on your optimized landing pages also benefit SEO. As with keywords in your paragraphs, ensure that your links fit naturally within your page and make sense to a real visitor. You should check that there are other pages in your site that link to the landing page using keywords wherever it makes sense.

Meta Elements

Meta elements are invisible to a reader but are visible to machines, and usually contain descriptions and keywords. With early search engines, they played a much bigger role; spiders were unequipped to deal with the huge computation overhead to interpret an entire web site, so they just looked to the meta description for an indication of the content inside. Nowadays, spiders are better at indexing content from pages—besides, some unscrupulous black hat webmasters would put false keywords in the meta elements to rank them in irrelevant searches if the old system still held sway.

Nevertheless, meta elements are still in use today, often as a piece of text underneath a search result. Spend about ten minutes formulating precise, tight meta descriptions and keywords, then move on.

Web Site Design Issues and SEO

Modern web design is becoming more complex while designers are continually pushing the boundaries with their designs. Here are some common issues that may trip you up if you're unaware of them:

Source Order

While the main content might look like the most prominent aspect on a web site, that content could be anywhere in the code. Often, unimportant content like sidebars appear first in the code, with the keyword-rich copy appearing later. A search engine spider disregards style, so when it interprets the content of a page it ignores any styling and will instead read the order of your content as it appears in the code.

Headings

It may be tempting for a copywriter to use a heading element to emphasize some text, even if it's just for decoration. Spiders, however, will still consider this to be a heading and will index that content accordingly, so you need to be careful about how you use headings. If you want to use a big, bold style for some standard text, ask your designer to provide you with a special class specifically for this purpose, and stay away from those heading elements.

Flash and JavaScript

Use Flash and JavaScript with caution. It's widely debated whether modern-day spiders are able to interpret content created by JavaScript. Flash content, on the other hand, can be indexed, but spiders fall short at understanding relevance and content. Even if they could do so, it would still be less accurate than interpreting real text on a page—so it's best to avoid relying on JavaScript or Flash to create content. If your designer must include these features, ensure that the technique provides a plain HTML fallback.

Content

Effective SEO copywriting is a craft that takes a lot of time, and involves trial and error, and a natural flair for words. You'll develop your own skill over time as you practise integrating your keywords into the text. A good way to approach your copywriting process is to begin writing the content of your page with total disregard for your SEO strategy; then, as part of your editing process, massage your keywords into your copy. The benefit of this process is that you're writing the copy for your visitors first, and then *gently* working in your SEO words. A keyword-stuffed page might look great to a search engine spider, but if the text is poorly worded or unclear, it can be quite unappetizing for human readers—and it's the humans who are spending the money on your site.

 Buy a Domain

For keywords with more traffic, you might want to check if the domain for that keyword is still available or for sale. No definitive proof exists to suggest that owning the domain will improve your ranking—but it certainly won't hinder it. In fact, it's more likely to attract a searcher's attention. Most of the keyword-rich domains have been snapped up already, but it's worth checking and grabbing it if you can.

Integrating Keywords into Your Content

The first step in either planning a new site or evaluating an existing site involves mapping your identified keywords into the content of specific pages on your site. To do this, first try to understand what the expectations a user will have when entering the particular search term. They may be looking for answers to a question ("repair rip in horse rug"), comparing different products or services ("best horse blankets"), or actually looking to buy ("cheap, extra large horse rug").

Once you've identified the expectations of your users, you need to decide what type of page to present them. There are basically five typical web pages:

1. **Information pages** are educational, answering a question or providing insight on a particular topic. Where you're selling a product or service they may act as an extension of your commercial site, attracting targeted traffic through free content, then funnelling it through to your products or services. A user might land here after searching on how to "repair a rip in a horse rug"—then be drawn to your advertisement for new rugs. Some searchers may have irreparable rugs, so it's the perfect time to sell them one.

2. **Summary pages** contain links to collated information. A summary page might be a list of a particular products, or links to categorized information pages. You may want to optimize your summary page so that it contains less specific search terms. For example, a searcher who enters the phrase "horse rugs for sale" would be well served by a summary page with options like style, color, or size.

3. **Product pages** are the sales pages for individual products or services. You would match these types of pages with customers who are ready to buy using specific search terms. For example, a searcher looking for a "blue, extra-large woollen horse blanket" would be best served by arriving on the appropriate product page—because clearly they're already sure what they want.

4. **Generic pages** are typical to most web sites. These include contact details, FAQs, technical assistance (for a product), and so on. Generic pages can often generate the most traffic. They are put up on a web site to help support a product but, with the right keywords, can be quite good at attracting search engine users.

5. A **homepage** is the top level of a web site. It contains links and pathways to other areas of the site. Homepages should be used for more generic search terms, as specific search expectations are harder to gauge for this type of page. You only have one homepage, so choose your homepage keywords wisely.

You'll find that most of the time, the most useful page for a visitor will be an information page. However, your most profitable pages will be your product pages. If your product or service can dominate the results in ready to buy keywords, you'll see a dramatic improvement in your online sales. Attracting ten visitors to your site who are ready to part with $100 for your product is worth much more than 1,000 visitors who are just browsing.

Short-term Gain, Long-term Pain

It's important to ensure that your content is useful and original. One easy way to acquire content for your site is to use **syndicated content**—articles that are free to reproduce on your site. While this may seem attractive (who would turn down free content?) these generic articles will never be as strong as your own, targeted articles.

Worse yet is **spam blogging**, or splogging—a black hat technique of grabbing keyword-rich content from other sites in the hope that it will inflate your site's ranking and attract visitors. This may seem tempting, but Google punishes this behavior by removing such sites from its index.

Duplicate Copy

One crucial problem to keep an eye out for is duplicated content. From the perspective of a search engine spider, reading and interpreting the same content over and over again on the same site represents wasted effort and resources. At best, the search engine will just stop indexing your content when it's had a few repeats; at worst, the spider may consider your content to have been created with black-hat techniques and subsequently ban your site!

It's almost impossible to eliminate duplicate content completely, but it's in a search engine marketer's best interest to minimize duplication. Try to avoid having more than one version of the same page. It's good to ensure that each title and meta element is unique too.

Tips for Spider-friendly Sites

Your site design needs to ensure that search engine spiders have a seamless journey while crawling your site. That way, the information a search engine collates about your web site is exactly as you wish.

Spiders are simple applications built for speed rather than complexity, and there are some simple rules of thumb to ensure your site is spider friendly.

Absolute Links

Spiders like links with the entire path (including the domain) better than they do relative links (without the domain). That is, links should look like `http://sitepoint.com/books` rather than something like `../books/`.

Titles and Headings

Your page title and headings are important for keyword optimization, but they also assist spiders to interpret your site. It's one of the first indicators a search engine will use as relevance for your content.

Updates and Changes

Tell the spiders when you make changes: Keep the search engines informed when you update your site. If you change your site to a new name or move pages around, you need to let the search engines know about it or you'll lose any existing benefit you had from your old pages. You can use **redirects**—instructions to web browsers and search engine spiders about where to go when a page has changed, and these can be temporary or permanent. Ask your server administrator about redirects.

Server Performance

Like humans, spiders have a certain level of tolerance with how long they'll wait for a web site to respond before moving on. There are many other (more important) reasons to have a fast-loading site, but poor performance will hurt crawlability.

If you can tick the boxes on all of the above, then your site will be crawling with spiders soon enough! If you're interested in looking at your site through the eyes of a spider, turn off JavaScript, images and styles in your browser's preferences, and you'll have a fair idea.

Popularity

When a search engine identifies two or more web sites with the same content relevancy for a search term, it will use secondary measures to determine which order to place them in the SERP. The amount of variables search engines use grows each year; however, the amount and type of incoming links you have to your site from other web sites plays a critical role in ensuring your site ranks higher than another.

Build Incoming Links

In the eyes of a search engine, if a web site is prepared to link to another site, it's a sign that the web site is credible. What's more, the text used for the link has to have some relevance: if a popular horse stud site links to your horse blankets site using the anchor text, "great horse blankets," then your site gains popularity and some added relevance for that keyword. The more incoming links you have pointing to your web site, the greater your overall site ranking will be.

These days, some links are more equal than others. In the case of Google, an inbound link from a high-ranking web site will have more significance than many links from low-ranking web sites. The number of links on the page, as well as where the link is in the context of the page's copy, can also influence a search engine's ranking of your site.

Fishing for Links: Linkbait

Creative, interesting content can be an invaluable source of generating inbound links. The most common approach is to produce **linkbait:** content that's interesting, useful, controversial, or funny. It can be anything that really grabs readers' attention and encourages them to post a link on their blogs, email it to friends, or share it on a social network. As well as being interesting or fun, a successful linkbait campaign can create numerous incoming links to your site and raise your profile.

A great example of creative link building is SlideShare,[8] a site for uploading and sharing slide presentations. A slideshow can be quickly translated into a widget that can be embedded and used on a third-party web site. Each time a user creates a SlideShare slide show and places it on their web site, a link is generated back to SlideShare. The more people that use the service, the more links they generate.

Free tools such as applications that can be embedded like this are often more beneficial in the long term than even the most controversial one-off linkbait content.

---

[8] http://slideshare.net/

Great Content Means Great Links

So what are the best links you can possibly hope to generate for your site? Ideally they'd have your preferred keywords in the anchor text that appears in the body of the content, and be found on a web site about a similar topic to yours, but with a higher search rank. While links like these this can be bought, they can also be earned. The way to generate quality links is to create quality content that people actually want to link to. It creates an SEO benefit and generates good referral traffic from the originating web site.

Buy Links

There are plenty of opportunities to buy one-way links from web site owners. You'll usually pay a monthly fee to the site owner in order to keep your link on the site, or pay for a one-time mention on a blog or news posting. The more popular the site, the higher the price you'll pay for your link.

If you do choose this route, be aware that this goes against some search engines' terms of service, and so you do run the risk (albeit low) of being excluded from the search engine altogether.

Link Exchanges

You'll find plenty of reasons to exchange links with other sites that complement your own. For example, a horse blanket store may exchange links with a horse stud selling actual horses. The two sites are relevant to one another, without competing against each other.

Directories

Directories are sites that contain collections of links to web sites, usually organized by categories. They are an easy way to gain one-way links. Some rank sites by quality and are moderated by real humans; others will accept any old site. Getting links from directories is probably the easiest way to generate a large volume of links, however the overall value of these links can be low. Links from related web sites are much better and should remain your number one priority.

Opportunity Knocks

There are plenty of ways to generate links to your site. Some of the easiest ones include:

- commenting on relevant blogs
- becoming involved in online forums who allow links in your auto signature
- distributing your press releases to online press release services
- submitting any article-worthy content to article aggregators
- offering your articles to social networking sites
- putting forward your web site to web directories
- creating a YouTube channel and video series
- referring your videos to video social networking sites
- using some of your best content as guest articles for other popular sites
- asking or answering questions on Yahoo Answers[9]

So there's ten easy ways to start the links flowing. Be careful to avoid being labeled as a spammer by stuffing keywords into blog comments and forum threads. Make sure you're adding value to the blog or forum.

You need to be opportunistic with linking. Use your network, develop thought-provoking content that's great bait for links, develop relationships with the media in your niche, work with government bodies and ask for a link. There are many creative ways to gain quality links back to your web site, but only if you remain the opportunist. Always be on the lookout for a little bit of link love. Before you know it, you'll have thousands of links back to your site.

Welcome, Spiders!

So you've set up your site, you've loaded up the content with keywords, and you're ready for the spiders to visit the site and build the index. How do you tell them you're open for business?

One way is to manually submit your site to search engines so that they know where your web site is. Most search engines have a contact form that allows a webmaster to enter some details about the site, including titles, keywords, or other information.

---

[9] http://answers.yahoo.com/

Spider Bait or Snake Oil?

Some developers claim to have created automatic submission software that submits your site to all the major search engines. The results of these applications can be unreliable. It only takes a short time to submit your site using the search engines' web forms, so you're better off to keep control of what's entered rather than rely on software.

The other way is through a link from a popular site. Popular sites are crawled frequently by spiders, so they'll pick up the link to your site in little time. Use the techniques described above to put your link out there—before you know it, a spider will be across your site and it's on from there!

Measuring and Tracking Success

A good search engine strategy is one that evolves over time. Rather than a set of predetermined rules, you need to evaluate what suits you best, and continually grow your search engine strategy. This includes all facets—from keywords to link building. To do this effectively, you must measure and track success on an ongoing basis.

Some important things to watch out for include:

- the search engine results pages for your target keywords—where do you rank?
- the number of incoming links, their anchor text, and the source's reputation
- other keywords that are generating traffic to your site
- your crawl frequency
- overall search engine traffic to your pages
- conversion rates of your search engine traffic

Record these metrics frequently so that you can analyse the effect that tweaks make to your campaign, from link building to copy and site layout alteration.

More on SEO

Engaging the Services of an SEO Expert

While this chapter will give you a starting point from which to leap into SEO on your own, you may find at some stage that you'll need to look to an SEO professional for assistance. The SEO industry has grown substantially over the last decade, and it's a quite competitive market. When looking to sign up with an SEO specialist (either an individual or organization), there are a few factors to consider, apart from money:

- proof of prior success with SEO (references)
- details of the plan they to intend to implement (and ensure it's white hat)
- independent perspectives on the specialist (search for testimonials about this person)
- recommendations from the SEO community

With the search engine industry, for the most part, you'll get what you pay for—but if it sounds to good to be true, it probably is. But I'd encourage you to seek out the best; there are a large number of top-quality, professional search engine specialists who are easy to find if you take the time to research.

The Future of SEO

What's next for SEO?

Links, PageRank, and the chase for the top spot on SERPs are so ingrained in the SEO industry—I think some people are actually addicted to their own PageRanks. The reality is that over the next few years the importance of building links will become so insignificant, it will stop being a major tool in an SEO professional's toolkit.

Search engines are becoming smarter and their ability to determine the relevance of content to a searcher's needs is improving every day. Relying on aspects like overall site popularity is becoming less of a necessity.

The actual dynamic of a search engine is evolving too. For example with Google, searchers are able to personally influence their own search engine results for future searches, geographical searching is becoming more precise, and behavior-based and intent-based searching is on the horizon. While the doomsayers claim this will be the end of SEO as we know it, I see it as a bright future, where there will be more to SEO than just links and keywords. Where quality content will reign supreme over black hat SEO, and the people producing the highest value will reap the search engine rewards.

Rest assured, though, that the benefits of a good link-building strategy are still healthy. As long as you take an interest in SEO industry news, you can adjust your strategies when and if there is a necessity to do so.

The Start of a Beautiful Friendship

Search engine optimization is a fast-paced, ever-changing industry and it's important to note that this chapter is just the beginning of your acquaintance with SEO. There are literally thousands of blogs, hundreds of communities, even local networking groups that you can be involved with to keep in touch with change—and they're just a web search away. Be assured that good SEO can generate healthy traffic to your web site, and excellent SEO will blow all your expectations away. Happy optimizing!

Social Media

The Internet has been a place for socializing since the early days of newsgroups and Bulletin Board Systems, AOL chat rooms, and the first online forums. But in the last few years, social web sites have sprung up that let us connect with more people and share more than ever before. As socializing in cyberspace meshes with real life—through notifications and updates to our cell phones and the ability to upload and post content on the go—more and more people will connect with friends, family, and colleagues over the Internet.

But the social web is more than just about talking to friends and family—it's a powerful marketplace where word of mouth can make or break products and companies. Unlike the marketplaces you're familiar with, ad dollars and fancy commercials lack currency in the social web universe. It works on a different set of rules: rules made by your customers, rather than advertisers or media companies. They decide what they watch and read, and who they listen to. We'll take a look at this new marketplace and examine ways you can use social media to connect with customers and potential customers, as well as build your brand.

What is Social Networking?

The phrase **social networking** may be a relatively new buzzword, but social networks have been around as long as civilization. The term was coined in the 1950s, when anthropologist J.A. Barnes used the phrase to describe the relationships between people in a Norwegian fishing village.[1] Social networks are just a way to describe our relationships with one another, and the interconnectedness of those relationships. We humans have always arranged ourselves into certain social groups—you're connected with other people through family, friendships, religious beliefs, financial status, education, political beliefs, and more.

The Internet brings people closer together than ever before, and allows people with like interests to easily connect even if they're thousands of miles away. As a result, social networking web sites have become increasingly popular over the last few years, with hundreds of millions of users worldwide.

What is Social Media?

Social media is a broad term to describe all the different kinds of content that form social networks: posts on blogs or forums, photos, audio, videos, links, profiles on social networking web sites, status updates, and more. Social media allows people with no knowledge of coding or web development to upload and post unique content easily and share with the world instantly. Simply put, social media is any kind of information we share with our social network, using social networking web sites and services.

Social Content Goes Mainstream

You might be thinking, "So what, it's just a bunch of kids chatting about the weekend or uploading goofy videos!" But social media is more than just about teenagers texting updates to Facebook[2] while they're in class. Social media is at the apex of a roller coaster; it has been gaining in users and momentum, and it's already making inroads into the mainstream. As such, its importance is growing every single day.

---

[1] Barnes, J. A. (1954). "Class and committees in a Norwegian island parish," in *Human Relations* (7), 39–58.

[2] http://facebook.com/

Social networks comprise more than your average geeks, with numbers of people using them up at an alarming pace. At the time of writing, Facebook claims over 175 million users worldwide—with more than 70% of those users outside the United States.[3]

In terms of growth, social networking is expanding much faster than the Internet as a whole. In 2008, social networking web site traffic grew 25%, while overall Internet traffic only grew 11%. Facebook grew 153% between June 2007 and June 2008[4]—and it's only heading up! And according to traffic analysis service, Alexa, social media web sites are solidly placed in the world's top ten web sites.[5]

So while social networks may have started out as the local geek hangout—just like the Internet in the 1990s—they've since been taken over by everyone, from college kids to business people to celebrities. News organizations, politicians, and even the President of the United States have embraced social media.

The End of Interruption Marketing

Twenty years ago, interruption marketing held sway. Traditional **interruption advertising**—television, radio, print, and billboards—are all designed to interrupt what you're doing and break your concentration. While reading an article you turn the page—and a full-page ad hits you in the face. You're at the climactic scene in your favorite television show when it cuts to a commercial. You're driving along a country road, admiring the scenery—and a billboard comes into view.

We all dislike being interrupted, and we've learned to tune out interruption marketing. You flip past ads in a magazine without even noticing them. You use commercial breaks as an opportunity to grab a snack, or fast forward through them with your video recorder, or watch your show online without commercials. But when people go online and socialize with other people, they actively participate in the conversation.

---

[3] http://facebook.com/press/info.php?statistics
[4] http://comscore.com/press/release.asp?press=2396
[5] http://alexa.com/site/ds/top_sites?ts_mode=global&lang=none

Social media allows you to talk to your customers directly, without all the marketing hype. You create the content and your customers—and prospects—will find it, read it, and discuss it because they *want* to.

Word of Mouth: Far Reaching and Fast

You may have heard that the most successful form of marketing is word of mouth. Customer testimonials are extremely powerful, and word of mouth has long been the most effective and least expensive form of marketing possible. When one of your customers talks positively about your company to a friend, it's free advertising!

On the Internet, word of mouth spreads faster than you ever thought possible. A good (or bad) customer review or comment can be picked up by search engines. Every time someone searches for your company, that review can be found. Now the review could be read by millions of people in a matter of days!

As people gather online in social networks, they are talking about your products and services, whether you like it or not. By becoming an active participant instead of simply the subject of conversation you can foster communication with your customers and increase brand awareness.

Grab the Opportunity

Social media right now is like the days of the gold rush of the American Wild West. There's so much untapped opportunity, because right now the space is inhabited primarily by individuals. Companies are only now realizing the opportunity to connect with customers, and the ones to get there first are grabbing the gold. Social networking is more than a fad; it's here to stay. The reason is pretty simple: people like connecting with other people.

Social media can be a powerful tool to help you spread the word about your products or services, but you have to participate in the conversation. The first step to participation is understanding the different types of social media.

Types of Social Media

Social media sites come in many flavors. Let's explore some of them.

Social Networking Sites

The most popular forms of social networking revolve around web sites such as Facebook,[6] LinkedIn[7], Plaxo[8], and MySpace.[9] These sites are built specifically for people to connect with others. Users start by creating user profiles that can include a biography, interests, photos and videos, notes, and even blogs. They can then use the site to find acquaintances, colleagues, friends, and family members, and list them within their profile as a friend, contact, or colleague.

Some social networks like Facebook and MySpace focus primarily on connecting friends and family, while work-based sites such as LinkedIn and Plaxo host resumes and professional information, connecting business colleagues.

Blogging

A blog—which derives its name from weblog—is a frequently updated web site that shows updates in reverse chronological order (newest at the top). These updates could take the form of journal entries, articles, or just cool links that people had come across. Some blogs can have as many as dozens of posts per day, while some blogs may barely post daily or weekly.

Blogs also typically have a category breakdown or archive, allow user comments, and offer content syndication through RSS. Even if you're unfamiliar with the term but have browsed the Internet in the last five years, you have most certainly come across a blog.

Blogs were previously the domain of individuals, or maybe a small group, but successful blogs such as TechCrunch,[10] Mashable,[11] and Lifehacker[12] have helped to

---

[6] http://facebook.com/

[7] http://linkedin.com/

[8] http://plaxo.com/

[9] http://myspace.com/

[10] http://techcrunch.com/

[11] http://mashable.com/

[12] http://lifehacker.com/

change the perception of blogs and push them into the mainstream. TechCrunch, for example, claims to have over five million subscribers.[13] By comparison, the print edition of the *New York Times* only has a circulation of one million.[14]

The lines are also blurring as to what constitutes a blog as opposed to a magazine-style site. While blogging was generally considered to be more of a short-form style, some blogs now publish full-blown, feature-length articles.

Microblogging

Microblogs allow you to post short updates, limited to very few characters, about your life, work, or anything. The updates are sent via instant message, SMS text message, or on a web site to people who follow your updates.

Microblogging services have been around a little while, but only recently have they experienced widespread mass adoption. Twitter[15] is the most popular microblogging service. Many larger social networking web sites, such as Facebook and LinkedIn, also incorporate a status update feature, which can be seen as a kind of built-in microblog of its own.

Microblogs can often be incorporated into web sites and blogs by showing the latest entry or a number of most recent entries.

Photo and Video Sharing

Web sites that allow users to upload photos and videos and share them with families, friends, and the general public are rapidly gaining in popularity. YouTube[16] has videos that have been viewed millions of times, even making some of the videos' creators (in)famous.

Previously, uploading and sharing media with others was difficult. Sites like YouTube became popular because they made it easy for anyone to upload and share their content online. Flickr,[17] one of the most popular photo-sharing web sites, has mobile phone applications for uploading photos from virtually anywhere. Users

---

[13] http://techcrunch.com/advertise/

[14] http://nytimes.whsites.net/mediakit/newspaper/circulation/nyt_circulation.php

[15] http://twitter.com/

[16] http://youtube.com/

[17] http://flickr.com/

can capture any moment and instantly share it with anyone or everyone. Users can search for photos based on a number of criteria, tag them with keywords, or aggregate them into groups. And like a social networking site, users of YouTube and Flickr can befriend other users of the service.

Bookmarks

It's tricky to remember that cool web site you found last week if you only bookmarked it on the office computer. Social bookmarking web sites can help solve that problem by providing a hosted and easily accessible set of your bookmarks. In addition, bookmarks can be shared with others and tagged, making it easy to find similar web sites or search for a specific topic. Delicious[18] is one such popular service.

Social News

Social news web sites such as Digg[19] gather links to news stories posted on web sites all over the Internet. The stories are submitted, rated, or voted on by users, and the most popular stories are featured on the site's home pages and and category lists. Another type of social news site is a blog aggregator, such as Technorati[20] or Alltop,[21] which categorize and display content from entire blogs instead of single posts.

Podcasts

Podcasts are audio or video recordings that you share online. Users subscribe to a feed of your program, which automatically grabs new episodes as soon as they're released. Podcasts can be created with digital video cameras and simple audio recording software, available for any operating system.

Video and audio can also be streamed live to the Internet through cell phones and webcams. Services such as Ustream[22] and Qik[23] offer programs for many different mobile phone models that can stream video live over the Internet.

---

[18] http://delicious.com/

[19] http://digg.com/

[20] http://technorati.com/

[21] http://alltop.com/

[22] http://ustream.com/

[23] http://qik.com/

Online Forums

Online forums are one of the oldest forms of social media, where people gather on web sites to have open discussions on niche topics. SitePoint has an online community[24] with more than 300,000 members and over four million posts about web development and online marketing. Online communities usually revolve around a specific topic such as sports, web development, or health.

The Social Media Mind-set

If you want to participate in social media, either personally or on behalf of your company, there are some things you need to know. There have been countless advertising agencies and PR firms that have created social media *profiles* to put out content on behalf of their clients, only to see a huge backlash from the very customers who use and love their products. Why? Because it wasn't genuine. And the reason why it lacked authenticity is because it breaks the first rule of social media: *be human.*

Being Human

One of the most common mistakes companies make when trying social media is that they maintain that corporate facade instead of behaving like normal, everyday human beings. Simply creating a Facebook page and Twitter account, then auto-posting updates from your RSS feed is an ineffective use of social media. I'd also recommend that you avoid running every post or update through the legal department, otherwise you end up with bland corporate-speak.

Social media connects *people*; to participate, you need to have conversations, the way real people do. If you're just posting marketing messages or uploading the same commercials you air on network television, that's just advertising. And if people have no interest in your advertisement on TV, it's unlikely they'll want to watch it on YouTube, either.

The key is to just be yourself. Leave the marketing hype and corporate-speak at the office, and just talk to people.

---

[24] http://sitepoint.com/forums/

Comcast's Human Face

Cable television companies are known to cop a fair share of criticism. Prices consistently increase, as do the number of commercials customers have to endure.

Comcast customer service manager, Frank Eliason wanted to know what people thought of his company, so he joined Twitter and started listening. Before long, he started replying to customers that tweeted their problems or frustrations. The response was amazing:

> I would like to state for the record that @comcastcares rocks. Fast and friendly service, and my new router is now up and humming! Thanks![25]

> @comcastcares delivered my new modem and now I have fast Internet again! Thanks for the great service![26]

Eliason has made quite a name for himself and Comcast customer service by simply being human and participating. He helps where he can, offering advice or connecting customers with the people at Comcast that can help solve their problems.

Starting Off with Social Media

So you want to make a start with social media, but you have no idea what to do or where to start? Let's take a look at the four steps to getting started with social media:

1. listen
2. join
3. participate
4. create

It's very important these are done in order—especially start with listening. If you were just recently asked to serve on the board of a major corporation, would you go into your first meeting with a list of recommendations for the company? That's unlikely—you could be viewed as a bit clueless and arrogant. Instead, you would probably go to a few meetings and learn what the issues were and what the other

---

[25] http://twitter.com/zaren/statuses/1211145208
[26] http://twitter.com/DavidLithman/statuses/1220931325

board members thought. Then, you might start participating in committees or discussions they were having. After building trust and learning about the company's issues, you could start making recommendations and voicing your own opinions.

The same is true for social media. When you join a community, you need to learn about how it works, including the rules—both written and assumed—and how to participate.

Step 1: Listen

This is the most important step. Online, people are already talking about your company, products, or brands. All you have to do is listen.

Even if you only do this one step, you will gain a huge benefit from social media for you and your brand. Companies pay hundreds of thousands of dollars to survey their customers, create focus groups, and other laboratory experiments which ultimately fail to provide any information about what customers really think—but you'll learn plenty simply by listening to what your customers are saying.

It's important to listen to what customers think of you, but just as necessary is listening to what they need and want. What are their problems? Frustrations? By listening to your actual demographic, you have an inside scoop on what's important to them. Keeping tabs on your customers and potential clients can lead to valuable insight into your products or services.

Back in Chapter 2 we showed you ways to monitor what people are saying about your company and brand online. Use those tools to find conversations about you, your market, and the other key players in your industry. Read blogs related to your products or services. Browse online communities related to your industry. As well as watching discussions about your company name or product, look for general discussions about your industry. For instance, if you were a cable television network, you might search for conversations about "cable TV," "cable," or even names of your competitors. Once you find blogs and web sites that have content you want to read, you can subscribe to updates using email or RSS feeds. There are conversations going on every day out there, and it's so easy to stay abreast of them.

Step 2: Join

Once you understand the lay of the land by listening, it's time to think about joining a social network.

You don't *always* have to join social networks to participate—you can often comment on blogs and post in forums as a guest—but many social networks require you to join to be a part of the community. Even if joining is unnecessary, it's better to join so you can claim your brand or company name and take ownership of your contributions.

There are so many web sites—how do you choose which to join? The first rule is join the communities where you find your customers participating. If you started out by listening—and I know you will—you'll already have a list of web sites that your customers are visiting.

Tips on Joining Social Networks

- *Use a memorable name*—Try to secure your own name or your company's name—unless another person beat you to it!
- *Use your real photo*—Company logos are okay for company profiles, but using a real photo of yourself is best. It's personal and shows that you're a real human being, instead of just a faceless PR spin doctor from Acme, Inc.
- *Post your contact information*—Even if it's just your company email address and office phone number, make sure people can contact you.
- *Be professional*—There's a large personal aspect to all social media web sites—but you should always be professional and remember you're representing your brand.

Which Sites to Join

As we learned above, it's a good idea to go where your customers are—but there are some popular sites that should definitely be on your radar regardless. Here's a list of sites that you should consider joining.

- Facebook: http://facebook.com/
- MySpace: http://myspace.com/
- LinkedIn: http://linkedin.com/
- Twitter: http://twitter.com/

- YouTube: http://youtube.com/
- Flickr: http://flickr.com/
- Delicious: http://delicious.com/
- Digg: http://digg.com/
- StumbleUpon: http://stumbleupon.com

The sites above are among the most popular, and cover a range of different purposes. There may be other sites you also want to join, but the above list is a great starting point.

Step 3: Participate

Once you have your bearings, you're ready to participate in the community.

Participation can include posting topics in online forums, replying to topics in forums and blog posts with your opinions, reviewing products or services, and even just bookmarking web sites you like. Here are some ideas to start you off:

- Blogs: Comment where you can add a unique opinion or your expertise.
- Online forums: Create discussions about important topics relative to your industry, and post insightful replies to other topics.
- Photo and video sites: Comment on videos and photos.
- Social bookmarking: Bookmark links, writing a concise description and tagging them appropriately. Comment on other links you find helpful. Share interesting links to other people's web sites that you come across.
- Social news: Post links to stories you find interesting, and rate stories posted by others.

By simply participating in the communities related to your industry, you'll help build your online brand. People will come to respect you as a valuable contribution to the community, and when you have news to share they'll help you promote it. After you've become a respected member of the communities, and you begin creating content, others will promote it for you, often without even being asked!

Spam Is Never Okay

It's so tempting when you first start with social media to treat it like a billboard, blasting out every special or promotion in an attempt to increase sales or revenues. This is often considered spam, and it's *never* okay to spam social media with your advertising! That means dumping links to your own web site, products, or services on other people's blogs or online communities, without any intention to communicate or participate.

While each community has its own set of rules (with some even allowing self-promotion), you'll go a lot further by simply making a contribution. Remember: *be human.* When participating in social media you should read the guidelines to see what's allowed and appropriate. Look at how other users, especially very active ones, are participating. If you have any questions about what's allowed or appropriate, ask an experienced user or a staff member.

Step 4: Create

Only after you've been reading, listening, and participating in other social networks, should you try to create your own content. By building an online brand for yourself—by way of contributing to the social networks and forming connections—you now have an audience to share your content with. After you've built that online brand and online reputation, you can leverage it to help spread the word about content you create.

Before we discuss how to create content, what kind of content should you create? Again, you have to provide value, and ads aren't usually considered valuable. No one wants to read a blog that simply advertises your product or service. Social networking is about making a worthwhile contribution. It's about community. Simply posting an ad to Twitter or a *buy my product* post on an online forum will fail to achieve the results you want—you may even be banned! By making a beneficial contribution to the community, people will notice and want to know more about you and your company.

But what sort of content should you create? That's hard to answer—everyone's needs are different. A pediatrician might start a blog with health advice to parents, while a music store might create video lessons on how to play instruments. In each case, they provide content in the form of advice to their customers—actual and potential—instead of advertising their products or services. Because you started out by listening to your customers and following web sites in your industry, you should already have a solid idea of the kind of content people want to see. That way, when you see an opportunity, you'll be ready to take it!

How SitePoint Gained 10,000 Twitter Followers in Two Weeks

When you first start out with Twitter, you might want to jump-start your followers list with a special promotion. SitePoint went from a relatively small following to one of the biggest on Twitter by running an exclusive product giveaway via the medium. The promotion was simple: users could follow sitepointdotcom on Twitter, and receive an eBook about CSS (worth $29.95) for free.

The campaign went viral, with widespread coverage both inside and outside of Twitter, and the number of Twitter users following SitePoint exploded. Since the book was about CSS, we knew that most of the followers we gained would be interested in the content found on SitePoint's web site. The momentum gained from this Twitaway resulted in continued growth, and SitePoint's Twitter count now exceeds 25,000 followers. You can read more about the SitePoint Twitaway at Twitip.[27]

Start a Blog

Blogs are incredibly valuable—they often act as central hubs for other kinds of media, like videos or podcasts, or as a link to your presence on social networking sites. What's more, they're a great avenue to create discussions through comments or posts on other blogs.

If you're just starting out with social media, creating a blog is an excellent way to begin. You can do it for free using a service such as WordPress.com[28] or Tumblr,[29] or install a blog software package on your own web site. WordPress[30] and Movable Type[31] are popular blog software packages, and there are many resources on the Web that explain how to set it up.

---

[27] http://twitip.com/how-to-grow-your-follower-numbers-to-over-10000-in-a-week/

[28] http://wordpress.com/

[29] http://tumblr.com/

[30] http://wordpress.org/

[31] http://movabletype.com/

Create a Social Profile

Most social media web sites allow you to create a profile page about you or your company (or both). These profiles give people a better idea of who you are and what your company is about. You should always be professional, but you can still include personal information, especially on social networking web sites like Facebook and MySpace.

Just remember, it's a poor idea to put up anything you wouldn't want your customers, clients, or the media to see!

Start Talking

Post updates, blog posts, photos, links, and news stories—and comment on others' contributions, too. The process represents a cycle rather than a one-time exercise: you'll frequently be monitoring web sites and looking for interesting content, commenting on it, and posting more substance of your own. People will begin to comment on material you post, and the cycle starts all over again.

Problems and Pitfalls

While social media can have a very positive impact on your brand, you should be aware of a few caveats before starting out.

Privacy

One of the most common concerns about participating in social media is privacy. People value their privacy, but a quick Google search can reveal all kinds of information about a person. Pulling information from multiple social media web sites and other sources can reveal a lot: names, birth dates, spouses and children, home addresses, job histories, and more.

Be aware of the privacy settings of social media web sites. Those that require birth dates only do so to verify age, and should allow you to make it private. A site should never require you to post a home address or phone number if you're uncomfortable doing so, nor supply sensitive information, such as a social security number. If you're concerned at all about your privacy, simply refrain from giving the web site any sensitive or personal information.

Transparency's Double-edged Sword

Transparency and openness are good, but completely unfiltered honesty can quickly turn sour. You need to practice common sense when posting to social media sites, even if it's using a personal account.

James Andrews found that out the hard way when he posted the following message to his Twitter account while visiting a client:

> True confession but I'm in one of those towns where I scratch my head and say "I would die if I had to live here!"

The city was Memphis, Tennessee and the client was FedEx.

Andrews may have been unaware that most FedEx employees, including the founder Fred Smith, are native Memphians and deeply love their city—and one of those employees was following Andrews' Twitter feed. The post quickly reached executives at FedEx and created a backlash against Andrews and the agency he worked for, Ketchum.[32]

Remember: when you post updates, opinions, and content to the Internet, even within your circle of friends, information can spread. Employees have been fired for posting inappropriate photos of themselves on their blogs or on web sites like Facebook and MySpace—it would be a difficult start to your fledgling social marketing efforts if the same happened to you.

Establish a Clear Social Media Policy

A company's employees should be very clear about what kinds of activities are acceptable, and this includes social media.

We discussed social media policies in some detail in Chapter 2. Use those principles to establish a clear social media policy that encourages openness, while also ensuring that employees are working to enhance and protect the good name of your brand.

---

[32] http://industry.bnet.com/advertising/1000525/worst-twitter-post-ever-ketchum-exec-insults-fedex-client-on-mini-blog/

Trademarks and Copyright

It should probably go without saying, but you should own the copyright to anything you post online, or obtain written permission from the copyright owner before publishing. Though you can usually delete content from social media web sites after posting, it may already have been reposted in other places—almost instantly. In fact, it may never truly disappear.

Let's Start Socializing!

You should now have a basic understanding of social networking, social media, and the ways you can start using them to help grow your business. We've seen how we can use different kinds of social media to have a conversation with our existing and prospective customers, and build your brand and online reputation. Most importantly, you've learned that the old ways of talking at your customers, rather than to your customers, are ineffective: the essential ingredient is to *be human.*

Email Marketing

If I were to add up all the revenue I've generated over the years and divide it by marketing channel, email would easily take the lion's share. What's great about email marketing is that it's one of the easiest types of marketing campaigns to carry out, the benefits are instant, and when implemented correctly the return on investment is substantial.

In this chapter I look at how a well-crafted email campaign is put together and run, and the methods used to manage your email lists and send messages.

Email's Undeserved Bad Rap

Email receives a bad rap. Businesses often shy away from running email campaigns in their marketing programs, as they're concerned they might be seen as spammers. Yet they're more than happy to have door-to-door salespeople and telemarketers represent them every day, where they lack any real control about the way those people interact with their potential customers—and it's never really made sense to me why.

Jeanne S. Jennings, in her email marketing bible, *The Email Marketing Kit* (Melbourne: SitePoint, 2007), provides one of the best summaries on the benefits of email marketing. I've paraphrased it here:

- Email is *cost-effective.* While there are costs involved in email marketing, such as copywriting and design, your production and delivery costs are significantly cheaper than that of direct mail. For the same amount, you can send out around a hundred emails for every direct mail letter.

- Email *builds relationships.* While email may not be the only method that helps connect you with your audience, it's the least intrusive— enabling the recipient to respond at their leisure. A well thought-out email plan can facilitate customer loyalty.

- Email is *"push technology."* Just like telemarketing, door-to-door, and direct mailing, email marketing pushes your message to prospective and existing customers, rather than relying on customers to seek you out first.

- Email provides *timely results.* The time between distribution and delivery of an email marketing campaign can be measured in minutes rather than days. This allows you to choose the time you deliver your messages with more precision, and also means results will become evident quickly after you start your campaign.

- Email is *quick to produce.* Once you're set up to run email campaigns, you can easily launch a major marketing initiative to all your customers in a few hours. There's no other direct marketing source that could be implemented in this sort of time period.

- Email *accommodates hyperlinks.* With just a little click of the mouse, a customer can go from reading your marketing message, to purchasing at your online checkout. This speedy, one-step process is what marketing dreams are made of.

- Email provides *detailed feedback.* Email marketing allows for comprehensive feedback. You can measure how many of your emails were successfully delivered and opened, how many times your links were clicked on and, importantly, how many sales you made. This also enables thorough campaign analysis.

- Email enables *affordable segmentation and targeting.* Email marketing is agile, allowing you to vary the content sent to customers on your distribution list. You can **segment**, or split your lists based on market segments such as geographic location, purchase history, gender, and age to send tailored messages, improving your conversion rate.

■ Email *plays well with others.* Email works well when part of an integrated direct marketing campaign. While other methods can come across as pushy or disruptive, email is able to prepare your customers for a sales call—or as a follow-up to a face-to-face sale—without getting in a customer's face.

■ Email can be a *viral marketing tool.* It's so easy for recipients of your email to forward your message to friends and family, quickly turning your small campaign into a viral bonanza.

Different Types of Email Communication

Email marketing is more than just sending out an email with a special deal on a product. There are a number of different approaches you can use to engage your audience, and each type of email communication sent will deliver different benefits to your business. Let's take a closer look at all of them.

Educational Communication

An educational style of message usually takes the form of newsletters, where knowledge is imparted on a regular basis. Let's say you run a Corvette spare parts store and you want to create a loyal customer base. Part of your offering might be to produce a free monthly newsletter which contains tips for repairing and maintaining your Corvette. First and foremost, editorial integrity must be preserved—it has to avoid looking like a sales push—however, there's still room to encourage readers to look into your products. Thinking of our Corvette example, each repair tutorial could easily come with links so that readers can order parts needed to complete the repair.

News and Updates

Keeping your customers up to date with what's new has never been easier than with email. One of the most effective ways to communicate news of important updates or changes to your business is to notify your customers via email. You might be releasing a whole new product range, changing your contact details, moving to another location, or announcing major changes to your web site.

Direct Sales Messages

Straight-up sales pitches are the big earners of the email group, where you communicate direct offers to your list. This can include offers on a single product, or catalogue-style emails with a range of offers.

Housekeeping

Housekeeping messages are emails such as subscription confirmation messages or welcome emails. These are often generated automatically by the system you use to send your email, but can be customized to your audience for greater impact. With some care and attention, these messages can be just as important to building relationships with your customers as your well-crafted direct sales email. For example, you could use a subscription confirmation message to thank a subscriber for taking the time to sign up, as well as showing off some examples of the great content they'll receive in the future.

Permission

If you want conversions with your email campaign, the key to success is to seek permission—that is, ensuring that the people who'll receive your email have chosen, and are expecting, to receive your messages. The likelihood of someone clicking on your link—instead of deleting the message—improves substantially when a user has opted in. That is, they've consciously chosen to hear those updates and messages from you.

We'll explore later in this chapter how to build your own email list, but in the meantime I really want to stress the importance of obtaining permission from anyone who's going to receive your emails. Otherwise, in most people's eyes you're going to be labeled a spammer. This will hurt your sales, your brand, and your business—and possibly create legal trouble.

Anti-Spam Laws and You

Laws are in place that govern email marketing and they vary across the globe. You should *always* make sure that you've read and understood these laws before embarking on email campaigns of your own. For example, many laws require that you provide an easy way for customers to opt out of future campaigns; another common requirement is you must provide adequate contact information in your emails. Failure to comply with these laws could wind up with you being blacklisted as a spammer.

Building Your Email List

There's little sense in devising an email campaign if there's nobody to send it to. Before you think about building campaigns, you need to start acquiring subscribers. Let's look at how you can add to your subscriber list.

News and Updates

Offer a "Sign up for news" option. Of course, the simplest way to obtain a user's email address is to ask if they'd like to receive news and updates. This can be in the form of an ongoing newsletter, a subscription to your press releases, or any other type of news from your business.

Ask Your Customers

When a visitor purchases from your site, ask them if they'd like to subscribe for offers and deals at the point-of-sale. While most spam laws cover permissions prior to a sale being made, it's still wise to avoid annoying your customers with unwanted email.

Giveaways

Think about offering a free product to a user who signs up for email. This is probably the most common source of acquiring email addresses beyond your customer base. Software companies offer trials or free versions of their software. Booksellers offer free sample chapters of their books. If you can offer an item or service for little or no cost, that provides value to a user, and your email list can build quickly.

Perks

In return for a customer providing their email address, you could offer premium or extended use of certain aspects of your site. This might be valued information, like tutorials, or it might be special offers on your products and services. A simple example would be running an online forum. A forum usually requires an email address for a user to join and participate in the community, so at the point of sign up, you could ask them to opt-in to your promotional material.

A Positive Call to Action

Regardless of what you're offering, you need to think about the text you use to encourage customers to sign up. Choose positive phrases that emphasize how your visitors will benefit from the message, with links like "Keep me updated on the latest news" or "Let us keep you in the loop about freebies and special offers!"

Offline Lead Generation

Email addresses are commonly only thought about online, but there are many opportunities to collect email addresses offline. Contact with potential and existing customers can occur over the telephone, over the counter in person, or in neutral territory such as workshops and conferences. Every time an individual talks to a representative of your business, it's an opportunity to add to your email list. One potential problem with collecting emails offline is that it usually involves an extra step to load those addresses into your email database. When looking for a technical solution on how to store your email lists, ensure that you're able to manually enter addresses, or import them from an external source such as an Excel spreadsheet.

Dangerous Shortcuts

You might be tempted to jump-start your email list by buying a list of addresses from a list broker. I advise against this as a starting point, as you'll just wind up spending extra money for addresses of people who've shown no interest in your product—and possibly tarnishing your reputation to boot.

will be messages from certain people you will open before others. This is why an aspect as simple as the name and address of the sender can have a great impact on the conversion rate of your campaigns.

There are two parts to the From field: the address (shayne.tilley@sitepoint.com) and sender's name (Shayne Tilley). While this might seem obvious to those used to seeing both fields, there are email clients that may just show the sender's name, and others, just the address. This is why it's important to consider both fields individually. The key objective of your sender details is to clearly present your identity using the least amount of characters possible. So an identifier like this:

Name: Updates

Address: 12342346323-updated@sitepoint.com

is basically ineffective, because neither the name nor address provide an indication of the company sending the email. On the other hand, this example:

Name: SitePoint Books

Address: SitePointBooks@sitepoint.com

achieves what's required: both the company and topic are clearly communicated in both the email address and name.

The personal touch of a real person's name in the From field increases your chances of the email being opened and read. Unfortunately, spammers have started to adopt this tactic too, so people are wary of opening emails from strangers. That means the best time to use a real name in the From field is when the recipient is likely to know the name of the person who's sending it.

Message Subject

This is my favorite part of creating my email campaigns. I often find myself tinkering with the subject line, hoping to stumble upon the magic formula. As with the From field, the message subject also influences a reader's decision in whether to read the email or delete it.

Your email subject line needs to indicate the type of message you are sending, so a direct offer will differ from a response to a transaction, or a system-generated message. The subject should communicate the main benefit of your offer in the fewest possible words. A good rule of thumb is to place all critical information in the first 20 characters with the subject no longer than 60 characters—this puts the most important information first, and ensures that your subject line is less likely to be cut off by a small screen.

When you're composing a subject line to indicate a sale or special offer, simply state upfront what's inside, for example:

- Free shipping on all Corvette car covers
- 10% off all stationery: this week only

If your message is a response to a transaction or a system-generated message, try to keep the subject line short and to the point. Make sure there is absolutely no ambiguity with your message:

- Your invoice for December
- Thanks for subscribing

Finally, for newsletter emails, you can have a standard subject line, a subject that summarizes the content in the message body, or a combination of both:

- SitePoint Tribune Newsletter for June
- Viral Marketing under the Microscope
- SitePoint Tribune: Viral Marketing under the Microscope

Message Body

Writing first-rate email copy is a skill best learned by reading and practising. To help you start, here are my top tips for great sales copy:

Opening Body Text: Start out with your offer and call to action. Your first two paragraphs should focus on these—you need to grab the reader's interest as soon as you can.

Middle Body Text: This is the meatiest part of your message, but it's important to make sure it's punchy and direct. When you're discussing a product, focus first on how it benefits the reader—that is, instead of just listing the features, explain the value your reader will derive from your offer. You can add a personal, conversational touch to your message by addressing the reader directly, using words like *you* or *your*. Most of all, try to be as brief as possible—eliminate unnecessary words. Keep your paragraphs to less than four lines, so that they're easy to scan.

End Body Text: Finish off with a strong call to action. If there's a way to remove any buyer risks, you should remind them of this now as well—for example, if you have a money-back guarantee.

Sign off: Sign off the email—and for some extra kick, use a P.S. to reinforce your call to action.

Format Correctly: Body text lines should be no more than 65 characters long when using a text format. If it's longer, use hard returns to shorten the line length. This ensures your email is easy to read and interpret.

There's a wealth of information on the Web about copywriting—be sure to check out Copyblogger's Copywriting 101[1] section for lots of tips.

You might consider hiring a professional email copywriter for your first few campaigns. While hiring a copywriter adds some cost to your campaign, the investment will give you a sense of the right approach to take with your email copy. Be sure to hire a copywriter who specializes in writing emails.

Avoiding Spam Filters

It's crucial that your message content avoids falling foul of a spam filter. Spam filters (also known as content filters) are a feature of most organizations' mail servers. A filter checks incoming mail against a set of rules and decides if the content resembles spam or contains unwanted information. Many of these filter systems will discard your message, and some service providers will even blacklist repeat offenders.

There are a number of automated tests available to determine if your message may be caught by a spam filter, as well as suggest changes you can make to reduce the likelihood of this happening. For examples, see Campaign Monitor's testing features[2] or MailChimp's Inbox Inspector.[3]

---

[1] http://copyblogger.com/copywriting-101/

[2] http://campaignmonitor.com/testing/

[3] http://mailchimp.com/features/power_features/inbox_inspector/

Once you have an idea of what the content filters are looking for, avoiding spam triggers will become part of your natural copywriting process.

Your Landing Page

On most occasions, the purpose of your email campaign is to gain clicks back to your site. It's important in any email campaign that you've thought about a **landing page**—the page a reader is directed to upon clicking the link. Landing pages can take various forms. In the case of a newsletter-style campaign, you might provide multiple links to related information on your site, while with a sales message, the landing page needs to direct users to the Shopping Cart containing the product or service on offer. Many marketers make the mistake of sending customers to a sales page once they've clicked on a Buy Now button. If you've sold the customer on the product via an email, there's no need to try and sell it to them again! The easier you can make the process for the customer, the more sales you'll make.

HTML versus Plain Text

There are two main types of email format: HTML format and plain text. Each has its own strengths and weaknesses and, depending on the type of campaign you're running, you'll need to decide early what format you're going to use. For my part, I run with a text-based format for sales campaigns and system messages, and both HTML and text for newsletter-based email campaigns. That said, I always try varying formats to ensure that conversion rates are maximized by the right format. So I might try the odd sales campaign in HTML, to see if more conversions occur. Here are some issues to weigh up when you're considering a plain text mail:

Pros	Cons
More informal and feels less like being sold to	no text styling (bold, fonts)
Low distribution overheads	Ugly links, not dressed up by text
Easy to read	Unable to gain "email open" rates
Low design costs	Lacks supporting imagery, such as product images or diagrams
Quick to produce	Limited layout capabilities
Consistent in all email clients	Less professional feel

On the other hand, you might consider a HTML email:

Pros	Cons
Attractive text styling (bold, fonts)	Less personable
Smart, clean links	Higher distribution cost
Statistics are measurable	High production cost
Option to include imagery	Slower to produce
Multiple layout possibilities	Inconsistency across email clients

In some ways, building a HTML email is more complicated that building a HTML web page. Instead of five or so main web browsers to cater for, there are dozens of web-based and desktop email applications you need to consider, each with their own quirks and restrictions on the kind of content you can send. If you struggle with the whole HTML and design caper, you may opt to have a professional design templates for you. Otherwise, you can use some of the tried and tested templates available for free at places like Campaign Monitor[4] or MailChimp,[5] modifying them to suit your needs. After you've made the necessary adjustments, use your campaign service's testing feature to check how your HTML email renders in the most common email clients.

When you run your first test, you may be surprised by how much variation you see. Different email applications treat emails in various ways. It's okay if your messages are subtly different—the time to start worrying is when the differences make your message illegible or non-functional.

Before You Send

The old adage to measure twice and cut once can be easily applied to email campaigns—once you've pressed the Send button, it's too late to fix any mistakes. Before you send a message, be sure to test everything twice. Set yourself up with multiple addresses on several free mail services, and then send your email to those addresses first, checking that your message is spot on. Once you've done your test, walk away

---

[4] http://campaignmonitor.com/templates/
[5] http://mailchimp.com/resources/html_email_templates

from your campaign for an hour or so and then test it again. You can never be too cautious with your quality checking and testing process.

Here's a quick checklist to use when you're testing your messages.

Content

- spelling and grammar are correct
- all links work
- the From, Reply, and Subject fields are in place

Design

- design is compatible with all major email clients
- email passes spam filter checks
- line length is correctly formatted

Distribution List

- the correct list is loaded and active
- unsubscribed customers are excluded or deleted

Let's Take a Breather

We've covered a lot already in this chapter, so let's take a step back and look at what we've discussed so far. Hopefully you now understand how email campaigns can benefit you, and how to start building your own email list. You're aware of some of the methods for managing the technical aspect of large email deliveries, as well as the types of different messages you can send. With all this wisdom, it's time to start planning your email marketing strategy.

Planning Your Email Marketing Campaigns

The first thing you need to do is complete a competitive analysis—that is, check out what your competition is up to. This is easy to do: your competitors should be actively building lists of their own, so you should have no trouble subscribing to their campaigns. If you spot any competitors doing a great job, you might want to order some of their products to gain insight on the kinds of messages they send to their existing customers, as opposed to their prospect list. This information will give you the inside edge on what your email campaign needs to do.

Best Times to Send

There are certain days of the week and particular times of the day when people are more likely to take the time to read emails. Ongoing industry research suggests that for business communication, Tuesday to Thursday are ideal days, and between 10.00 a.m. and 3.00 p.m. is the ideal time. However, other markets may differ, so ensure that you test different approaches and see if there's a better time. For instance, you might find that if you're promoting a computer gaming product, people will be more receptive to these messages outside work hours—that's when they're more likely to be thinking about leisure activities.

You also need to remember that in this global economy, your customers could be in many different time zones. If it's possible, it's a great idea to segment your recipients by time zone and send emails based on the recipient's time and day, increasing the likelihood that your email will arrive at a good time to read. Some email campaign services will allow you to schedule each group in advance, so that you can reach each zone of your audience at the best time.

Segmentation: Targeting Your Emails

As your email list grows, a key to ongoing success is segmenting your lists into specific demographic groups to improve the quality of your conversion. Using what you know about the people on your list, carve it up into smaller batches and run email campaigns directed to them. Your first port of call might be your customers' purchase histories, allowing you to focus your promotion on products of interest to them. On your subscription form, you might wish to offer your members the option of HTML or text email, and then ask for a few details about them, such as gender and geographic location. When they eventually make a purchase, you could use the opportunity to ask whether they're using your product for home or business. These are all legitimate ways to gain information so as to tailor your campaigns to your audience, providing a greater chance of eliciting the desired response for each kind of subscriber.

Sequencing

Email is often considered to be a one-hit wonder among online marketers. You have an offer, you put in an email, you send it out and then you wait to see how many sales you make. This, however, is a very shortsighted view; email marketing is about a growing, evolving relationship with each customer. That's why limiting your campaign to one email could be restricting your revenue—instead, consider sending a **sequence** of messages.

When I'm sending direct emails in a campaign, for the most part they'll be made up of a sequence of two or more emails. For example, say you have a special offer of a 20% discount on a product for an entire month. To make sure your recipients have every opportunity to hear about it, you could try a sequence of three messages. The first message would be sent at the start of the month, announcing the amazing deal and letting subscribers know it finishes at the end of the month. The second email could be sent a week before the end of the month, reminding people that there are only seven days remaining to take advantage of the sale. The final email could then go out on the last day, telling customers that it's their last chance to snap up a bargain.

By running multi-email campaigns, you'll double the conversions of a single hit. So when the offer dictates it, think about running your campaign in phases.

Frequency and Scheduling

When planning your email campaigns you'll need to decide what to send out, and how often to send them. This needs to be done at a global level with all your email messages. While you might think of your sales messages as separate to your system-generated housekeeping messages, to your customers they're all still notifications from your company. You risk annoying your subscribers if you bombard them with three emails in a day; as opposed to three emails in one month. There's no golden rule on how many is too many, as it can depend on the kind of business you're running. You'll need to find the right mix as you gain a better feel for the tendencies of your customer base.

Once you've considered each of these issues you'll be able to develop a schedule of your email messages and campaigns. This allows you to share your plans with others, which is important if other departments within your company have a stake in your email campaign.

A simple schedule may look like this:

Email	Type	Frequency	Format	Sequence
Monthly invoice	System message	Monthly (1st day of month)	Text	No
Monthly sales offer	Direct sales	Monthly (1st Wednesday of the month) with a seven-day follow-up	HTML	Yes
Weekly newsletter	News	Weekly (Tuesdays)	HTML	No
Specials	Sales	Bi-weekly (2nd and 4th Thursdays)	HTML	No

Measure, Test, Optimize, and Refine

As I've mentioned throughout the chapter, there is no one-size-fits-all formula for email marketing. What I hope I've taught you are all the important factors you need to consider to find what works for you. Measuring at every stage, looking at alternatives, and testing variations are critical when pursuing your options.

The more you investigate what's working and what's not, the quicker you'll improve on the revenue you generate from email marketing. A careful re-evaluation of all the ingredients of your email marketing campaigns will be often forgotten, or done only sporadically, and it's too easy to focus solely on the sales outcome. Be warned that in the case of email marketing, failure to measure, test, optimize, and refine will often lead to underperforming campaigns.

Where to Find More Information

Email marketing is fun and extremely profitable. The problem is that it sucks you in—fast. You'll soon find yourself with thousands of customers on your list, and ready to take your email program to the next level. For further reading, I strongly recommend you take a look at Jeanne S. Jennings's *The Email Marketing Kit*, available from SitePoint. I refer to it as the email marketer's bible and recommend it highly.

Affiliate Marketing

Imagine hiring a group of independent sales agents to generate referrals for you. You'd only have to pay them a commission for referrals that make a sale, and you could sit back and concentrate on the stuff that really matters.

If that sounds good to you, affiliate marketing is a weapon you should add to your arsenal. In this chapter we'll talk about how affiliate marketing works, why it's good for your business, and how to set up and successfully run your own affiliate program.

The most popular outcome in affiliate programs is when a sale of a product or service is made, however other tasks could include a prospective lead generated though an email capture form, a phone call, or even a meeting appointment. You only pay a commission on outcomes from leads the third party has delivered, and the actual transaction is still completed on your own site.

What is affiliate marketing?

An affiliate marketing program is where you enter an agreement with third parties who'll promote your product on your behalf, and send traffic to your web site. In return, you'll pay some sort of bounty when a visitor they've delivered completes a certain task on your web site. Referrals are usually made to your site through the use of a button or a special kind of link on an affiliate's site. When a user clicks the link, your system picks up on that fact and records any subsequent activity—usually, a sale—as having been referred by that affiliate.

Affiliate marketing programs have been a part of the Web since the mid-nineties. Two of the best examples of affiliate marketing schemes that helped build commerce-based web sites into billion-dollar businesses are those run by eBay[1] and Amazon.[2] These schemes have contributed significantly to the rapid growth in the popularity and revenue of these online giants, and would easily be the most favored among publishers of online material.

There are two sides to affiliate marketing: the merchant or vendor, who has a product or service for sale, and the publisher who generates leads to them. In this chapter, we'll focus on managing an affiliate program as a merchant.

What are the benefits of affiliate marketing?

Affiliate marketing is an attractive option for a number of reasons.

Fixed Return on Investment (ROI)

In most affiliate programs, you either make payments after a sale, or your payment is made up front, however your price per unit is always fixed. And because you only pay for sales that are made, your **return on investment**—the amount you make compared to the amount you spent—is predictable.

---

[1] https://ebaypartnernetwork.com/
[2] https://affiliate-program.amazon.com/

Extending Your Reach

Affiliate programs enable you to expose your products or services to new prospects beyond your usual reach. You're also able to leverage the brand strength of your affiliates to help improve your own image.

Time to Stay Focused

If you can develop a large affiliate base that sends plenty of quality traffic to your site, that's one less task you have to concentrate on. We covered this in Chapter 2, and if you're short on time or resources, having a group of affiliates working with you can alleviate some of the work of generating leads, allowing you to focus instead on converting those leads to sales.

The Risks and Pitfalls of Affiliate Marketing

Of course, there are some risks involved with affiliate marketing, which you should weigh up carefully when you're deciding whether to dive in to affiliate marketing.

Losing Control of the Marketing

An affiliate's objective is to send quality traffic to your site. In order to do this, they'll use all the marketing tactics described in this book. This includes email marketing, on-site advertising, search engine marketing, and so on. As a result, you lose some direct control on how your web site is being represented to potential customers. Affiliate marketers might use tactics that you're uncomfortable with, or may even be directly competing with you for advertising space. You can enforce some restrictions on the affiliate's marketing techniques through the agreement you put in place with the affiliate; however, it needs to be closely managed. We'll go into more detail on how to manage your affiliate agreements later in this chapter.

Doubling Up on Leads

You might find that your affiliates are sending you traffic that would have come to your site anyway—and you're *paying* them for it! It's an inevitable symptom of a widespread affiliate marketing program, and it can certainly make you wonder why you would bother paying another for sales you could have made regardless. While there might be a bit of an overlap, your affiliates may also have the time and expertise to drive sales profitably in places unavailable to you—so on balance, putting up with this can be worth it.

The Risk of Fraud

With any affiliate program, there's a risk of exploitation. It's almost inevitable that you'll experience some kind of attempt to exploit weaknesses in your affiliate program. Keeping meticulous records and ensuring that your system has fraud detection features built into the system will help you identify fraudulent behaviour quickly, before the damage is done. We'll explore these shady tactics in a later section.

Types of Affiliate Web Sites

All kinds of web sites can use partners to generate an income, rather than sell a product or service themselves. Let's use the gaming industry as an example.

An ecommerce store selling boxed computer games would be a prime candidate to run an affiliate program. For this example let's assume that they ship physical products around the globe. Sites that would be a good fit for their affiliate program could include:

- general game reviews sites
- gaming forums
- gaming blogs
- tips, cheats, and walk-through sites
- sites offering trial downloads
- discount coupon web sites

All of these types of sites might offer insight on one specific game, or might cover multiple games.

You might wonder why these sites don't just sell the games themselves. One reason is that the site owners are more likely to be enthusiasts—and they're generally more interested in talking about the games, rather than dealing with customer shipping issues, credit card charge backs, or warehousing. In most cases, it's a perfect way for them to create an income without these logistical pressures. As the retailer, you're able to take care of that for them and share some of the rewards.

Another good source of potential affiliates could be sites that sell a complementary product to what you sell. To continue with our gaming example, a site might offer a printed guide on a particular game. The guide and the game ideally go together, so an affiliate program benefits everyone.

Ingredients for a Great Affiliate Program

Affiliate programs can deliver massive income—numerous online millionaires have made their fortunes doing exactly that. Successful affiliates are very astute business people who'll only spend time on programs that make them the most money. You need to make sure that you're giving them the tools to help drive traffic to your site, and you have plans in place to convert that traffic into sales. If your program fails to deliver, there are plenty of others worth trying. Here are some basic questions that top affiliate marketers will ask.

Is there a fit between my audience and your product?

There needs to be a logical fit between an affiliate's audience and the products or services you provide. If their audience is simply uninterested in your products, even the best advertising or direct marketing campaign will fail.

What does your site look like?

Just as your web site needs to look credible in the eyes of your customers, your affiliate program needs to convey the fact that you run a professional operation, capable of turning the leads they send you into sales. Affiliates might be interested in joining your program if they like your commissions or brand, but if your site's design suggests that it would fail to convert visits to sales at a reasonable rate, they'll quickly move on to alternative programs.

How well do you communicate?

Will you keep your affiliates up to date about the latest products and services you're offering? Are they going to be the first to know about new opportunities to make referrals? Do you encourage feedback? Successful affiliate programs treat their affiliates as partners, and so should yours. Later, we'll talk about ways to keep in touch with your affiliates.

What is your ad creative like?

Busy affiliates lack the time to build **advertising creative**—that is, the images, text, and other material that forms an advertisement—to place on their site. They will look to you to provide a range of top-class material that will seamlessly integrate with their own site. You need to ensure your creative caters for a cross section of formats and styles, including image-based and text-based formats. Creative will also need to be consistently updated to stay in line with any new promotions, seasonal events, or changes in product offerings.

How established is your program?

In the eyes of affiliate marketers, age can equal credibility—to some degree. A lot of affiliate programs and networks have come and gone over the years, and many marketers have been left out of pocket. It's a barrier you'll need to work hard to overcome if you're just starting out with your own program.

What's your tracking interface like?

Affiliate marketers are some of the best statisticians on the Internet. They'll run multiple campaigns with different programs at the same time, and optimize their own advertising based on results. You'll need to make sure your program offers a complete statistical package such as clickthrough and sales rates, or sample download counters.

How easy is it to implement and maintain campaigns?

Once they're approved as an affiliate, how quickly can they start running? You need to make it simple to generate their affiliate links, grab the ad creative they need, or copy code to help them make a start. There are so many good, easy-to-use affiliate programs out there—why would they waste time with an overly complicated process?

What's the agreement? What are the Terms of Service?

What limitations does the program place on affiliate marketers as partners? What are their responsibilities? If they have a large newsletter following and your program excludes any email marketing activity, they will look elsewhere.

What's your minimum payout?

In an affiliate program, the **minimum payout** is the amount of earnings a participant should have made before you process the payment. A low minimum can be attractive to an affiliate, as the lower the minimum payout, the sooner an affiliate can access their earnings. Having said that, a quick payout could also make your program more attractive to fraudsters—if they can grab the cash quickly and run, you have less time to catch them out.

What's your payment method?

A good choice of payment options is very important to an affiliate. You need to provide a variety of payment methods for your partners to choose: a good start is to ensure that PayPal, cheque, and wire transfer are among them.

Under the Hood

It's important to understand the technicalities involved in putting together an affiliate program so as to make the right decisions when setting it up.

The most popular type of affiliate tracking mechanism is implemented using cookies. A **cookie**—a small text file—is created on the user's browser when they visit a web site. In the case of an affiliate system, these text files contain details of the referring affiliate and the date of referral. These cookies are placed when a user visits the affiliate program's web site from a special link—for example, they might follow a URL from *http://example.com/number1affiliate*.

When this page is loaded, the cookie identifies that person as having been referred through *number1affiliate*, with the date of their visit. Then each time this customer orders a product, their computer is checked to see if an affiliate cookie is present. If there is a cookie, the sales lead is credited to the affiliate.

While it's an imperfect solution—people might use multiple computers, or turn cookies off—it's widely accepted in the affiliate marketing community to be the best practice we have.

When setting up your program you'll need to decide on an expiry time frame for the cookie. An affiliate program with cookies that's valid for 60 days will have a lot more appeal to an affiliate than one that is valid for only 30. You'll also need to make a decision on how to handle conflicts between affiliates: say, for example, an affiliate refers a visitor to your web site but no purchase takes place; then the following day the same visitor is referred from a second affiliate and then makes a purchase. Do you credit the sale to the first or second referrer?

Beware of Cookie Stuffing

Wherever there's a way to make money, there's usually someone trying to scam the system, and affiliate programs are no different. One method of exploiting an affiliate program is by placing tracking cookies on people's computers without them knowing, let alone having visited the actual affiliate web site. This exploit, known as **cookie stuffing**, has been used against large affiliate programs like eBay, and shady affiliates have earned thousands of dollars in commissions for sales that they never referred to the site directly.

This kind of activity is illegal and should be explicitly mentioned in your affiliate program's terms of service. Tools which help unscrupulous individuals conduct cookie stuffing are becoming more complicated and secretive, so it's worth looking out for. Affiliate marketing service providers such as Commission Junction[3] are consistently on the look out for such suspicious behavior.

Choosing an Affiliate System

There are three main ways to run your affiliate program, each with their own benefits and pitfalls.

Build Your Own

The first is to develop your own internal capability. This is a very tall order if you're just starting out, as there are a number of technical challenges and business rules you need to cater for in an affiliate system, which are difficult to identify right at the beginning. You'll need to spend the time developing your own system, or hire a developer to do this for you.

Buy One

The second option is to buy affiliate software and integrate it into your web site. This has the advantage of keeping complete control over the process while avoiding the hassle of building the application from scratch—you simply configure it to suit your needs. There are a number of quite good out-of-the-box solutions, such as iDevAffiliate.[4]

---

[3] http://cj.com/
[4] http://idevdirect.com/

Use a Service Provider

Finally, there are affiliate service providers who will run your affiliate program end-to-end. The largest example of this is Commission Junction. The main benefits of using an affiliate service provider is that they have all the systems and infrastructure in place, including an existing base of top-quality publishers ready to start promoting your products. Service providers will also use their extensive experience in combating affiliate fraud to help you minimize your risk of exposure. The downside to this option is that they'll take their own cut of the commission, which will reduce your profit per sale. Think about this carefully though, as the cost of your time to manage the administrative aspects of a program can often exceed the fee affiliate programs will charge.

Which should you choose? All three options have their strengths and weaknesses, and which option you choose needs to come down to your technical resources and experience, desired profit margins, and the amount of time you're prepared to spend on setting up your affiliate program. Both building and buying your own system comes with a certain amount of ongoing upkeep well beyond the setup. You'll need to collect identifying paperwork from each affiliate that joins. You'll need to keep detailed records of all the transactions and audit all the commissions. You'll have to respond to all the customer service enquiries from affiliates that want to know your policies, when you pay out, or how to use your user interface. You'll need to keep on top of bugs and improvements. These costs can quickly add up.

So if you're starting from scratch I recommend using a service provider. It's the quickest, most hassle-free way to start running your program.

Your Commission Model

At the heart of your program is the payment model you put in place for your affiliate partners. The type of commission you choose to pay can vary depending on the type of products/services you provide. The most common type of payment is a percentage of the total product sale amount (excluding shipping and taxes). A fixed amount per product sold is also common, however this can eat into your earnings down the track if you're applying any discounts to products—so the fixed model makes more sense if you plan to pay commissions for noncommerce-based activity, such as lead and appointment generation.

Bonuses and Incentives

Added incentives are a great way to enhance the attractiveness of your commission model. You may wish to include added incentives or rewards in your payment model, to attract large affiliate partners and retain successful ones. These incentives could include bonus payments when a certain volume of sales is achieved, or a different commission percentage when specific performance levels are met in a month, or a combination of both. For example:

Monthly Sales	Commission—% of total sale amount
1–9	5%
10–49	7%
50–99	9%
100+	10% + $500 bonus

Other examples might include bonus payouts during promotional periods to ramp up activity, or flat-rate payouts for a new product launch. You may even wish to offer prizes rather than additional payouts. As we were writing this book, AzoogleAds[5] launched a competition to encourage improvement: affiliates who brought in the most traffic in a three-month term compared to the previous period would be invited to a party at the Playboy Mansion!

Prompt Payment and Outstanding Accuracy

Nothing sours an affiliate program quite like a problem with payment. Credibility can make or break an affiliate program. If you're starting up, it's imperative that you've covered all of your bases in terms of data accuracy and payment process. Affiliate marketers using a new system will be on the look out for any gaps in processes so, early on, your program will be under the microscope. Chances are your new affiliates will have been burned before by programs that never paid out, or strange discrepancies in record keeping. Place yourself in the affiliate's shoes and only launch a program that you would be comfortable with yourself; if you trust your own system, there's a better chance your affiliates will too—otherwise they'll jump ship quickly, before it costs them too much money. Be prepared to adequately

---

[5] http://azoogleads.com/

explain why a sale was excluded or a commission was reversed due to fraud, or other sources, errors, returns, or any other reasons. Questions that go unanswered will only further frustrate an affiliate.

You'll also need to ensure you're timely and accurate when you pay your affiliates. For some people, income earned through affiliate programs is a major part of their livelihood, so delays can be painful. Can you imagine what would happen if you delayed your salary payments to your staff for a couple of weeks? You should feel the same level of responsibility with your affiliates. If your program develops a bad reputation for payment, it's a hole that's very difficult to dig your way out of.

An easy way to achieve this is to ensure that your affiliate has instant access to your sales data, so that records can be updated as soon as a sale is made. This allows affiliates to access their stats in real time and avoids any confusion. You'll also need to use some sort of accounting package, such as Quicken or MYOB, to quickly and accurately compile affiliate data and turn it into payment information. Using applications like Excel to manage payments might work early when your program is small, but as it grows, this will become more and more troublesome.

The Affiliate Agreement

An affiliate agreement acts as a set of rules that govern the relationship between you and your affiliates. As well as covering what they can and can't do, it should also state what you're committed to do for them. It should cover what are considered acceptable marketing practices, details of how sales are attributed to an affiliate, approval processes, exclusivity, agreement duration, processes for severing the relationship, payment terms and methods, and much more.

If you're using an affiliate service instead of rolling your own solution, one great benefit is that their affiliate agreements have already been put in place many times over and it will just need to be tweaked to suit your particular needs.

If you do need to draft up your own terms, you need to both employ the services of an experienced affiliate contract writer and have the terms independently reviewed by your own legal counsel. Unfortunate as it is, there are people out there who'll attempt to exploit your affiliate program, so you must have a strong agreement in place that protects you and your affiliates. The agreement won't eliminate fraud on its own—you'll still need to police it—but it will provide you with grounds to act should you discover any malicious activity.

Recruiting Affiliates

The world's best affiliate program is useless if people are unaware of it—so you need to champion your program. Launch your affiliate program like you would a new product. Create a press release, promote it on your own site, and use your social networking presence to spread the word—this book's full of ideas, especially in Chapter 2. If you've signed up to an affiliate service provider they're already helping you to promote your program, so you'll already have a head start, but it's still worth putting in the effort—you might be able to negotiate a space in their newsletter for the first month or three, or be a featured listing in your category. If you can conjure up some strong, early momentum, organic promotion of your program will begin to take care of itself.

In addition to this, you should start marking a target list of potential affiliate partners. Start by conducting a web search on your industry, and create a list of the higher ranking sites. Investigate each one's suitability for your affiliate program and start contacting them one by one. It's best to avoid approaching a web site that sells competitive products—instead, target content-based sites which are more interested in communication than in selling products or services.

 Dealing with Bigger Sites

Some larger sites may want to negotiate a higher commission to promote your products to their audience. Approach the negotiation like you would a bulk purchaser of your product: how much volume would your business need in order to reduce profit margins by 5%, 10%, or even 20%? Will the sales be mostly new customers? Will they be higher value sales? These are all considerations in your negotiation process that will ultimately decide how much extra you'll pay a large affiliate—if at all! Make sure you get in writing the full marketing efforts they're prepared to undertake. Sure, they might have a dominant market position and a large audience, but why give away some of your profits for nothing?

Working with Your Affiliates for Shared Success

Whenever an associate mentions to me that they've set up an affiliate marketing channel and it's underperforming, I ask them what they're doing to help their affiliates generate more leads. In most cases I'm faced with a blank look.

One of the common traps for new affiliate marketing programs is that they're set up, a few affiliates sign on, some revenue comes in the door, and then it's left to trickle along with minimal communication to the affiliates. These semi-abandoned programs are destined to suffer a slow death over time.

Right at the start of this chapter I mentioned that an affiliate marketing program is like employing a whole team of sales agents; would you hire a group of sales professionals but stop short at giving them the information and advice they need to help do their jobs better? You need to remember that your affiliates are in a partnership with you. They help you extend your reach and gain new leads, and the better they are at doing that, the more money you'll make.

A great way to keep your affiliates informed and up to date is through a monthly affiliate newsletter. This gives them a single reference point to keep on top of what's happening with your program. If your program grows enough you might consider extending communication channels to include private forums, blogs, and so on—but keep it simple to start with.

Here are some ways of keeping in touch with your affiliate group to help generate those extra sales.

Keep in Touch about New Products

If you're about to launch a new product or make changes to an existing product, make sure they're the first to know. You might even throw in an additional incentive or reward to help build some momentum with the new product.

Share Your Creative

Provide them with your best advertising copy and artwork. If you launch a new advertising campaign and you discover that one type of advertising creative works better than another, make sure you let all your affiliates know.

Share Success Stories

Share others' success stories: if you have an affiliate who's had a great month, ask them to share their success tips with others. Have them talk about what they did differently and share it with the rest of the group. As well as reinforcing that there's big money to be made, it will increase the performance of your entire affiliate group.

Of course, if there's an element of your own campaign that's been extremely successful, share this with the group too. You might have run an email campaign with a certain pitch and subject title, and it converted well. Let others use this angle with their own audience.

Seek Feedback

Encourage feedback—directly and through surveys or polls—to discover if payouts are right, ad creative is good enough, and how you could improve.

Research Your Competitors

Whether you're just planning to launch your affiliate program or are already established, it's always a good idea to see what your competitors are up to. It's great if you're lucky enough to be in a market without a standout program in place, prime for the picking, but in most cases you'll find you have some competition. Sign up to your competitor's program to see what sort of payment structure they have in place, what sort of application they're running, and what artwork they provide, and … well … make sure your program's better. Searching through affiliate networks is another way to determine average payouts and terms. Most of your target publishers will be exposed to these programs, so the need to be competitive is paramount.

You also should ensure that your research is more than just a once-off exercise—keep on top of new tactics your competitors and peers are using.

If a competitor starts losing affiliates to your program they'll react, and that's when the fun of a competitive market really begins.

Summing Up

You should now have an understanding of what an affiliate program is, and the ingredients that make up a well-run program that's geared for profit, as opposed to a poorly run program that will cost you more money than it will make. We've seen how to grow your affiliate marketing program over the long term by keeping in touch with your affiliates, providing great incentives, and staying on top of the competition.

An effective affiliate program can really boost your sales and your profits. It can take your products to entirely new markets and, best of all, requires little or no initial investment. That said, it's not easy, and requires attention, particularly in its early stages. And while there'll be other online marketing programs that you'll need to set up for your business, this is one that should never go off your online marketing radar.

Chapter

Online Advertising

You've undoubtedly seen many forms of online advertising. **Online advertising** is a blanket term that covers a wide array of marketing forms like banner ads, search engine marketing, popups, and video ads.

This chapter focuses on the main forms of online marketing—search engine marketing, social networking web sites, and on-site marketing—and discusses the planning, implementation, testing, and optimization of online marketing campaigns.

What's up with traditional advertising?

Back in Chapter 5, we touched on the idea of **interruption marketing**—a form of advertising that disrupts what you're concentrating on, like a TV program or a magazine article, to draw attention to itself.

Think of some of the situations where different forms of traditional marketing *interrupt* you so that you can see their message:

- A billboard appears roadside while you're driving down the highway.
- You turn the page to keep reading an article only to be confronted by a full-page ad.
- The television station switches to a commercial break.

Traditional advertising is all about interruption. Interruption marketing can work, but people have become so inundated with marketing messages that we've learned to tune out. The average person sees several hundred advertisements per day, so after a while they start to all look the same. As we learned, this form of marketing is becoming much less effective as people learn to ignore these kinds of ads.

Television, radio, and print advertising are hurting, partly because of the expense involved. Full-page ads in popular magazines can cost tens of thousands of dollars per issue, while television and radio commercials are expensive and time-consuming to produce. It can also be difficult to target segments accurately with traditional media, where a more general approach is required. So does that mean offline advertising is going away? Perhaps not …

The Good and the Bad

Although a lot of advertisers are cutting back on overall advertising spending, traditional advertising media still has its place in the world and seems unlikely to go away anytime soon. Print advertising can be very influential for timed offers, like sales and promotions. Television and radio can be useful for building brand awareness for your company or product.

However, advertisers these days want to know more and more about the effectiveness of their ads, and that can be tricky to determine with traditional media. How do you know if a walk-in customer saw your ad in a newspaper or heard you on the radio? Which radio or television ad worked best? An increase or decrease in overall sales is an unreliable measure if you're using more than one form of advertising at a time. There are ways to track the source of sales from offline advertising, but it's nearly impossible to do this instantly, or without extensive market research.

Supplement Your Online Campaigns

Traditional advertising can be useful as a supplement to your online marketing campaign. For instance, business cards, brochures, flyers, and mail-outs are effective marketing tools when used at the right time in the buying process. Once a prospect has visited your web site and requested more information, sending supplemental literature is appropriate and can significantly increase conversions.

Split Up Your Marketing Budget

If you want to continue with your offline marketing efforts, try splitting up your budget—reallocate some of your marketing budget to online advertising and continue with offline marketing in parallel. But as you're able to track the effectiveness of your online marketing campaign, you'll likely move more and more of your marketing budget into online advertising.

How Online Ads Are Better

Online advertising is rapidly gaining in popularity. It can be targeted specifically to the people looking for your products or services when they're ready to buy, and it can be measured to ensure it's working.

Measurability

The biggest advantage of online advertising is in how easy it is to measure its success. Online advertising gives us the ability to track clicks and sales, and determine the number of leads or sales, as well as the cost of every conversion.

There is an old saying: "knowledge is power." When set up and configured properly, online advertising can provide you with a wealth of information; you can use this to determine your campaign's effectiveness, and make changes accordingly. You can see which ads performed well and which ones flopped. You can run tests to determine which of several headlines was the most effective, and by how much. You can evaluate and improve your campaigns regularly, making them more and more profitable.

Highly Targeted

Online advertising can be targeted to a very specific audience: it's easier to ensure that your ads are shown only to the market segments you're interested in. For example, you can target visitors of a specific web site who have similar interests to your customers, or you can show advertisements on search engines for terms that relate to your product. Relevance makes online advertising much more useful for the consumer, and so is more likely to convert them into customers.

Permission Marketing

In his blog, Seth Godin coined the phrase **permission marketing**, which he defines as "the privilege (not the right) of delivering anticipated, personal, and relevant messages to people who actually want to get them."[1]

Permission marketing is much different from interruption marketing. Instead of interrupting a person's day, you connect directly with people who are looking for your product or service. They want to find you and read what you have to offer.

Online advertising is a combination of interruption and permission marketing. Banner advertisements would be considered interruption marketing, while search engine advertising comes under permission marketing—because a reader will only click it if they want to see what's behind the link. With online advertising there's an increased opportunity to use permission marketing alongside interruption marketing, depending on the needs of the campaign.

Interaction

Television is a passive, one-way medium. No matter how loud you yell at your television, those commercials are still going to play—unless you've shelled out for a TiVo. Advertisers design and create ads and push them out to consumers without any instantaneous communication, interaction, or feedback.

By comparison, online ads allow you to interact with potential customers. They can click your ad, browse your web site, and request more information without having to remember a phone number or drive to the store. This opens up a whole new medium for advertisers to connect with potential customers. In addition, online

---

[1] http://sethgodin.typepad.com/seths_blog/2008/01/permission-mark.html

advertising allows you—the advertiser—to gauge the response of users and adjust your marketing promptly for increased conversions.

Standard Advertising Attributes

Online advertising is full of acronyms and industry-specific words that will be covered in this chapter. Ultimately, when terminology is put aside, advertising boils down to three different sections: the ad media, distribution, and payment.

Types of Ads

Web content is flexible and, of course, so are the choices of ads. Let's explore the most common types.

Display Ads

Display ads, or banner ads, are images that contain a marketing message and link to your landing page. Banner ads have been around since 1994, when AT&T advertised on HotWired with a banner that read: "Have you ever clicked your mouse right HERE? YOU WILL."[2]

 Standard Banner Sizes

The Interactive Advertising Bureau (IAB) publishes a list of standard Web banner ad sizes on their web site.[3] At the time of writing there are 17 standard ad sizes—that's a lot to keep track of! To keep it simpler, I'd suggest you stick with the standard sizes defined in the IAB's Universal Ad Package,[4] which consists of the four most popular banner ad sizes. Many online publishers have agreed to support at least these four ad sizes. It's good to concentrate on the most popular advertising sizes, as it means a publisher can easily find a spot on their page to accommodate your ad.

Text Ads

Text ads are any paid advertisement that uses hyperlinked text to link to a landing page. Text ads are typically comprised of a title, a short description, and a link.

---

[2] http://commercial-archive.com/content/banner-ads-tenth-birthday
[3] http://iab.net/iab_products_and_industry_services/1421/1443/1452
[4] http://iab.net/iab_products_and_industry_services/508676/508767/UAP

Rich Media or Flash Ads

You've most likely seen a rich media ad—some of them can be really annoying. These ads are usually created in Flash or JavaScript, and can feature video, interactivity, and even gameplay.

Video Ads

A video ad is a form of display ad that when clicked, plays a video. There is usually a call to action in the video, and clicking again takes the visitor to the ad's landing page. Video ads are excellent ways to show product reviews or demonstrations.

Popups and Popunders

Popup ads open in a new window on top of the current browser window, while a popunder appears underneath. Sometimes popup ads (and popunder ads) are just image or video ads, but they can take other forms. Popups can be full web pages, and can include video, rich media, or a contact form.

Ways to Purchase

And if you'd had enough of the amount of terms and acronyms already, the advertising industry has come up with a way to confuse you even more! There are several different ways ads can be displayed to visitors.

CPM—Cost per Mille

Under the cost per mille model, you pay a flat fee for every thousand impressions, regardless of whether your ad gains any clicks or conversions. CPM has been a common fee structure for some time. Just to add to the confusion, Mille sounds like it might be short for million, but it's actually the Latin term for a thousand.

CPC—Cost per Click

CPC click is the cost per (each) click of an ad. With this model, you only pay when a user actually clicks your ad and is taken to your landing page.

CPA—Cost per Action

CPA is the cost per action. With this model, you only pay when a web site visitor completes a designated task, such as signing up for a free trial or making a purchase. CPA is sometimes referred to as Cost per Conversion or Cost per Acquisition.

Now that we've covered some of the industry-specific terminology, let's look at the most popular form of online advertising: Search Engine Marketings.

Targeting for Better Results

Competition in today's online marketplace is intense. Search for any major product category and you'll see what I mean: shoes, toys, MP3 players. Whether directly or indirectly, online advertising goes to the highest bidder. By targeting your online advertising, you'll have a better chance at campaign success.

The Importance of Targeting

The goal of **targeting** is to ensure your advertising is shown specifically to people who are likely to be interested in your products or services. Targeting increases your chances that the viewer will take the time to act on the ad, while lowering your per-customer acquisition costs.

There are people who'll never buy your product or service because they won't ever need what you offer. Quite simply, they will never become your customer. That's what we call an **unqualified** person, and another goal of targeting is to save money and effort by knowing how to *avoid* marketing to those people.

How do you use targeting in your online advertising? There are many different types of targeting, and some types can only be used with particular forms of online marketing.

Keyword Targeting

The most popular form of targeting for online advertising is **keyword targeting**. There are two main ways keyword targeting works in online advertising. The first is through search engine keyword marketing, in which you can target ads to visitors who are searching for specific keyword phrases. For example, if you were to use keyword targeting for a Chinese restaurant in London, you could choose to show your ads to people who searched for "London restaurant" or "London yum cha."

The other type of keyword targeting is **contextual**. Ads are displayed on a page based on the keyword phrases that appear in the content. For example, a blog post that mentions a visit to a yum cha restaurant in London would be a good place to display your ad.

Demographic Targeting

Demographic targeting allows you to choose particular groups of people based on a number of criteria. Depending on the web site or ad publisher, you may be able to target your advertising based on the following criteria:

- age
- gender
- marital status
- income
- language
- interests and hobbies
- other demographics

Behavioral Targeting

Behavioral targeting uses information from **cookies**—small pieces of information stored on your computer for web sites you visit—to track browsing trends such as pages visited or searches made on search engines. Large web site publishers use behavioral targeting to display ads across their networks.

However, behavioral targeting can be applied to an individual web site. You can track browsing behavior or search trends using cookies, and offer advertisements based on articles or products that the visitor has viewed in the past.

Identifying Past Visitors

Identifying and targeting past visitors is a form of behavioral targeting. Using cookies, you can determine if a visitor has accessed your site before and even where they originally came from (such as a search engine or directory).

By using this information, you can tailor the experience to those users. Returning visitors are often looking to make a purchase after reviewing your offer, so you might make the call to action more prominent.

Geotargeting

Geotargeting—short for geographic targeting— allows you to display ads relating to the reader's physical location. Using the visitor's IP address or even the domain name they access, you can determine with degrees of accuracy where they're from, down to the city, state, or province.

Geotargeting can be extremely effective when marketing a business with local reach. By limiting your marketing to only the geographic area of your customer base, you ensure that you only receive visitors that are physically able to become customers.

Determining What to Target

Knowing about the different types of targeting is only half of the battle. Another major part of targeted advertising is understanding which criteria you should use for your targeted advertising campaigns. Here are a few tips.

Look at Your Current Customers

Look to your current ordering trends for information about your customers. Are they predominantly women or men? Do you notice any trends in age range, income status, location, or other factors?

Survey Your Visitors

Using a service like SurveyMonkey,[5] it's easy to place a simple survey on your web site. You can also send email surveys to current or past customers.

By collecting basic demographic information, you can begin building a profile of your customers. You can also log the IP address of your visitor, like an online street address, which offers additional information about their location.

---

[5] http://surveymonkey.com

Industry Data

Look at industry reports from companies like Forester[6] or First Research[7] for information about your target demographic.

 Too Choosy?

Targeting is extremely important, but try to avoid being carried away by it. If you target too tightly, you may be expending a lot of time and expense for a group that's too small to give you any meaningful benefit.

Advertising on Search Engines

One popular way to expose your advertisements to a large audience is to place advertising on search engine results pages—usually above or beside the actual search results. Search engine advertising targets visitors who are searching for the types of products or services you offer. When precisely targeted, search engine marketing can be extremely effective at generating traffic and leads.

Where to Advertise

Google, Yahoo, and MSN dominate the search engine market. Combined, they control over 92% of global search traffic, according to a February 2009 report by ComScore.[8] Because Google has such a large market share, a simple rule of thumb when determining which search engines to place advertising with is to start with Google AdWords. As you tweak your ads and your budget grows you can add Yahoo Search Marketing, Microsoft adCenter, and others.

I'd steer clear of splitting your marketing budget evenly among the top three, as that would leave you spending two-thirds of your budget on less than one third of the market. Instead, start with Google AdWords. As you add other search marketing companies, do so in the order of market share (for example, Yahoo, then Microsoft adCenter) and take note of the market share below when determining how much to budget for each.

---

[6] http://forester.com/

[7] http://firstresearch.com/

[8] http://comscore.com/press/release.asp?press=2750

Search engine	Marketing program	Market share	Suggested budget
Google	Google AdWords	63.3%	$700
Yahoo	Yahoo Search Marketing	20.6%	$200
Microsoft	Microsoft adCenter	8.2%	$100
Total Marketshare		92.1%	$1000

In addition, splitting your efforts across two or three systems requires duplicated efforts, which could be spent optimizing your campaign for best results.

In the rest of this chapter we'll spend most of our time talking about using Google AdWords, since it has the largest market share. Of course, the principles are the same for other services.

Organizational Structure

All of the top three search engines organize advertising in a similar way, though their terminology varies a little. Accounts are segmented into campaigns, which break down further into ad groups. Each ad group can target a specific set of keyword phrases. This allows you to segment your campaigns into groups targeting specific customers.

Campaigns and Ad Groups

Just as you would target a print advertising campaign to certain newspapers or magazines, campaigns and ad groups allow you to target your ads to specific groups through keywords and location targeting. You can set a budget for each individual campaign, and track each one's effectiveness from your Google AdWords account.

Creating Your Campaign

You should create a unique campaign for each broad category of products or services you offer. For example, if you sell electronics you might choose to use the following campaigns:

- personal computers
- portable computers
- home theater setups
- GPS units

With Google AdWords, location and language targeting is done at the campaign level. If you need to target several different demographics you would create multiple campaigns. For instance, if you ship your home theater goods nationally, but also provide a home installation service to local customers, you might choose to split up your home theater campaign, like so:

- home theater goods, targeted to your country
- home theater goods and installation services, targeted to a particular city

Creating Ad Groups

Ad groups break your campaign down even further, allowing you to target specific keyword phrases for several different ads. You can create multiple ads in each ad group, and one set of keyword phrases. Using the example above, you might choose to break your laptop computers campaign down into several ad groups:

- desktop replacements
- gaming laptops
- sub-compact notebooks
- Apple laptops
- HP laptops
- Dell laptops

Ad groups allow you to break a campaign into very specific niche segments, which will allow you to target your ads directly at those search engine visitors. In Google AdWords, you can create up to 25 campaigns per account, each with 100 different ad groups.

Selecting Keywords

Once you have your campaign and ad groups created, you need to target those ads using keyword phrases. Starting with the search engine optimisation (SEO) keywords we made in Chapter 4, we'll expand on those keyword phrases.

The More the Merrier?

The more targeted keyword phrases you have at your disposal, the better! When optimizing your web site for an organic, or natural, search engine ranking, you can only optimize for so many phrases—as there's only so much space on each page of your web site. Trying to optimize for too many phrases would reduce the effectiveness of the most important ones.

Search marketing is different. You can choose hundreds of targeted keyword phrases for multiple ad groups without diluting your effectiveness. In fact, if they're all equally targeted, you simply increase your ad's reach and therefore its effectiveness.

In addition, Google AdWords rates your ads' effectiveness—also called a quality score—which impacts the price you pay for each click or conversion. The more targeted your keyword phrases, the better your quality score and your conversion rate.

The Long Tail

Coined by Chris Anderson, the term **long tail** describes that part of the market that's outside of the mainstream—and it's big! Companies such as Amazon[9] and Netflix[10] are perfect examples of this strategy. They carry thousands of niche titles that are impossible to find in bricks and mortar stores; as Anderson's article points out, more than half of Amazon's book sales come from outside its bestseller list.[11]

In search engine marketing, the long tail refers to targeting many specific targeted phrases (instead of broad generic ones) to catch those niche queries. Targeting a generic phrase such as "horses" would yield visitors looking for all kinds of horse-related products, services, and information—plus, your ad will probably be competing with many other horse ads. By creating very specific keyword phrases, you can

---

[9] http://amazon.com/
[10] http://netflix.com/
[11] http://wired.com/wired/archive/12.10/tail.html

increase the chance of conversions because you can limit the number of people that view your ad, ensure that your ad is relevant to those viewers, and keep those who are uninterested from seeing it.

Choosing Great Targeted Phrases

The tools below will all help you find keyword phrases that may have failed to cross your radar. For example, typing "shoes" into Google's keyword tool brings back phrases like "men's shoes," "discount shoes," and "wholesale shoes." The keyword tools also provide you with information on the approximate search volume of the keyword phrases. You can gain more information on estimated clicks using the Google Traffic Estimator, which can show you approximately how many impressions and clicks an ad will receive before you start creating your campaigns.

- Google AdWords Keyword Tool[12]
- Google AdWords Traffic Estimator[13]
- Wordtracker's free keyword suggestion tool[14]
- SEO Book Keyword Suggestion Tool[15]

Phrase Matching

In Google AdWords, there are several ways to match keywords to search phrases:

- *Broad match*, the default option, simply matches all the words in your phrase that were in the search phrase. For example, if your keyword phrase was "shoes," your ads would appear on searches for "men's shoes" and "women's shoes" as well.
- *Phrase match* targets specific phrases. "Running shoes" would still be displayed to a user searching for "men's running shoes," as opposed to a "shoes for running" search. Phrase match keywords should be enclosed in quotation marks.
- *Exact match* only matches your keyword phrase as it is.

Phrase match and exact match are highly targeted and generally preferred, but there are reasons to use broad match keyword matching. If you're advertising a general

---

[12] https://adwords.google.com/select/KeywordToolExternal
[13] https://adwords.google.com/select/TrafficEstimatorSandbox
[14] http://freekeywords.wordtracker.com/
[15] http://tools.seobook.com/keyword-tools/seobook/

product in a small geographic location, you might use broad match keyword matching but geographically target your ads to only display in your local area.

Negative Keywords

Negative keywords combine with broad match or phrase match keyword phrases to limit the number of searches that display your ad. For instance, if you sell running shoes except women's shoes, you should add the negative keywords "women" and "women's." That way, your ad will appear for searches on "running shoes" and "men's running shoes" but exclude searches for "women's running shoes."

Looking at your web site statistics is an excellent way to find new negative keywords. By looking at the search engine phrases that people use when they click through to your site, you'll notice words that you can exclude from future ad impressions, increasing your ad's effectiveness and saving you money.

Think about all the possible broader terms that are inapplicable to your product or service. These are good choices for negative keyword phrases.

Writing an Effective Ad

Writing effective ads is a combination of science and marketing skill. Like a recipe, there are things you simply have to include. But other aspects are subjective and are better tried and tested first.

Anatomy of a Text Ad

Google AdWords text ads comprise three main ingredients:

1. Headline—up to 25 characters
2. Body—two lines, up to 35 characters each line
3. Display URL—up to 35 characters

Editorial Restrictions

With Google AdWords, you're forbidden to use all capitals or punctuation to draw emphasis to your ad. You may not have more than one punctuation symbol in sequence, and proper spelling and grammar are required. Additionally, ad claims must be verified on the ad's landing page.

Below are a couple of examples of ad headlines that would be rejected:

- Download a FREE Guide
- Buy Widgets Today!!!

Writing an Effective Headline

Headlines should be concise. Use simple words and include keyword phrases wherever possible. The headline should spark visitors' interest, and provide the solution to their problem. Below are some tips for writing a headline that attracts clicks:

- Apply the same keyword phrase you chose for this targeted campaign. This conveys to a reader that you have what they're searching for.
- Employ positive, instructive calls to action, such as *buy*, *download*, or *find out* instead of uninformative phrases like *click here*.
- Exploit brand names. If you sell a brand name product that is recognized and well received, using the brand name in your title can add credibility.
- Use the idea of scarcity to your advantage. Limited quantities, expiration dates, or other urgency factors reinforce the idea that the reader should look at your offer right away, in case they miss out.
- Utilize third-party validation. People may be reluctant to trust you, but social proof is a powerful thing. If you earned five stars or a best in show, use it to your advantage.
- Quantify the advantages. Numbers and statistics are more believable than generic statements. If you say your product is faster, how much faster? If it's less expensive, how much will they save?

The Body of Your Ad

With only two lines at 35 characters each, you have to convince the prospect that out of at least ten search engine results and up to ten sponsored results, they should click on your ad. To do that, construct a brief and memorable **unique selling proposition**—why should they choose you over the competition? What makes you better?

Below are some ideas that can form part of your unique selling proposition:

- guarantee or warranty
- free shipping or instant delivery

- experience or expertise
- range of product or service offering
- specialization in a niche market

Your ad can contain partial sentences or clauses. While incorrect grammar and broken English are disallowed, coherent sentence fragments are perfectly fine. Think of the types of headlines you might see in a newspaper, and consider the following:

- Best in Show Two Years Running
- Free Shipping on All Orders
- 24/7 Phone Support
- 365-Day Return Policy

The Display URL

You might be tempted to simply use your actual landing page URL as the display URL, but you'll gain more value for money by tweaking it to include keyword phrases or action words. Then, redirect that URL to your actual landing page.

The Google AdWords policy states that the domain on your display URL has to match your landing page URL, but that's all. For a more effective landing page URL, use a short, concise address without page extensions. Also try to include the keyword phrase. Here are some examples of great display URLs:

- example.com/super-widgets-sale
- super-widgets-sale.example.com

Notice the lack of visual noise, such as www, .html, or .php.

All of the three largest search marketing companies highlight search phrases in their results. This means that including keyword phrases in your ad text can add visual interest to your ad, attracting attention.

Designing Display Ads

Display ads (banner ads) should generally follow most of the same general guidelines as text ads. They should have a clear and concise headline and a call to action. The benefit of display ads is that you also have the ability to add visual impact to your message. But display ads are unique also. They can come in different sizes, can be animated, and may include colors and graphics that grab attention.

Size of the Ad

As we learned back in Standard Banner Sizes, there are many different sizes of display ads: from small squares to large rectangular leaderboards, display ads are very diverse. They can be static images or animated like a movie.

In most cases, as with Google AdWords, you'll be limited to certain sizes for your display ads. You'll need to choose between them based on:

- graphics you plan to use in your ad
- your logo's orientation or size
- ad copy and headline length

Ad Copy

Writing interesting display ad copy is similar to writing good text ads—but instead of a limit on the number of characters you can use, you're limited by size. Keep your copy short and your headlines shorter.

If you have several things to say in your ad, consider using animation or frames to split the message into short segments. You still need to keep the segments and the number of frames short and concise.

Design and Graphics

The design of your ad should fit with your overall branding. Keep the colors and fonts consistent with that of your landing page or company web site.

Generally speaking, avoid loud colors and flashy animations. They may gain people's attention, but they can negatively impact your brand and decrease conversions. The exception is if your company or web site colors are bright and loud. Primary colors work well for eBay, where the corporate colors are primary colors, but might be less successful for other types of organizations.

Obnoxious ads are noticed, but it will be clear to the viewer if the ad is congruent with your brand and product—or not. The overall goal is for your ad to be *clicked*, rather than just noticed. To do both, include visually engaging graphics in your ad. Consider including:

- product graphics
- company or product logos
- lifestyle photography

Ad Formats

The ad publisher (such as Google AdWords) may allow you to submit ads in multiple formats, such as JPG, PNG, GIF, and Flash. Which format you use will depend on how your ad's composed:

- With solid colors or text, use PNG or GIF. These formats allow for crisp, clear outlines and color.
- If featuring photographs or gradients, use PNG or JPG. These formats provide smooth, clean gradients.
- For animated ads with mostly solid colors and text, use an animated GIF.
- If animated in frames with photos or gradients, use Flash instead. The GIF format copes poorly with photos and gradients.
- More than 5–10 frames of animation or interactivity should use Flash. The Flash format allows for extended animation times and interaction.

A Few Tips for Effective Display Ads

- Have sufficient contrast between the ad background color and any text, so the ad is clearly legible.
- Simple is better. Avoid adding too many elements (text or graphics) that may distract a viewer from the overall message of your ad.
- It's a very poor idea to use graphics resembling operating system windows or dialog boxes. You might receive clicks from confused readers, but your conversions will be slim and you could have your ad removed for violating policy.

Limiting Yourself with a Budget

Search engine marketing can grow out of hand quickly without setting a reasonable budget. But how do you know where to start? There are several factors to consider when setting a budget for your campaign.

Available Funds

Advertising costs money, so your current cash flow will be a factor when deciding your advertising budget. Look at your current marketing budget to determine how much you have available for online marketing. If you've yet to establish a marketing budget, look to your monthly profit and loss statements to determine how much you can afford to spend.

Estimate Your Conversion Rate

If your web site is already generating leads, you can estimate your current conversion rate by dividing the number of **unique visitors**—that is, the number of individuals visiting the site—by the number of conversions, and multiplying that by 100. The resulting figure is expressed as a percentage.

(Number of conversions ÷ Unique visitors) × 100 = Conversion rate (%)

For example, if you have 2,500 unique visitors to your web site in a month, and your web site generates 100 sales:

(100 ÷ 2500) × 100 = 4%

Using industry reports—such as Coremetrics' Benchmark Industry Report[16] or FutureNow's "Top 10 Online Retailers by Conversion Rate" reports,[17]—you can determine the average conversion rate for your industry. This will give you a good idea of what to expect. Our next step is estimating your traffic.

Find Your Maximum Cost per Click

The **maximum cost per click** (CPC) is the maximum price you should pay per click, at a fixed conversion rate, to remain profitable. Your maximum cost per click will change as your conversion rate changes.

To determine your maximum CPC, multiply the gross profit per order by your conversion rate.

Gross profit × Conversion rate = Maximum CPC

---

[16] http://coremetrics.com/solutions/industry-report.php

[17] http://grokdotcom.com/2009/03/18/top-10-online-retailers-by-conversion-rate-february-2009/

If you sell a product that costs $100 and makes you a $25 gross profit per order:

$25.00 × 0.04 = $1.00

As you can see, your estimated maximum cost per click to remain profitable is $1.00 with a 4% conversion rate. If your conversion rate was 2%, the estimated maximum CPC would have been $0.50 per click.

Estimate Your Traffic

Once you have an idea of your conversion rate and maximum cost per click, it's time to estimate your campaign's traffic. Using the Google AdWords Traffic Estimator Tool,[18] enter your keyword phrases and location targeting preferences, such as your preferred regions or languages, then simply put your estimated CPC from above as the cost per click. Leave the daily budget field blank.

The Traffic Estimator Tool will display estimated clicks and cost per day. If this amount is acceptable, then create your campaign and set that amount as the daily limit. If it's too high, that's good! That means as you become successful, you have room to grow and expand. Simply lower the daily budget to a limit you are comfortable with for testing purposes.

You should have a high enough daily budget that with your estimated conversion rate, you should gain several conversions per week. You need enough data for your results to be statistically significant, so you can track metrics and use them to improve your ads and conversion rate.

Launch Your Ads

Once you're comfortable with your campaign and ad groups, keyword lists, landing pages, maximum cost per click, and daily budget, you're ready to start advertising!

Before You Launch

Before you launch your campaign, go back through each ad group, set of keywords, and landing page to review. Make sure your daily budget and maximum cost per click are correct.

---

[18] https://adwords.google.com/select/TrafficEstimatorSandbox

Also, be sure to test each ad variation by clicking on the URL or title, confirming that the web address is correct and that the landing page loads. Test the landing page, including filling out any forms or purchasing a product. Make sure there are no errors, misspellings, or problems in the process. Ask a friend to look over it for any obvious mistakes you may have missed.

It's Go Time!

Launching your campaign is usually almost instant. Ads will begin appearing within minutes in most cases, and impressions and clicks will begin to show up on your dashboard.

After Launch

When you first begin your campaign, resist the urge to tweak your ads. It takes time to collect useful data, and any change to your ads or landing page can skew your statistics.

Google AdWords conversions and Analytics data can take 24–48 hours to process, so you'll have to be patient for at least that long before viewing any real data on the effectiveness of your campaign.

Reviewing Your Campaign

Reviewing your search engine marketing campaigns should be part of your daily or weekly routine. Learn more about reviewing your campaign metrics, and how to optimize your campaign in the next section.

Online Advertising Metrics

One of my favorite movie quotes is "Show me the money!" from *Jerry Maguire.*[19] Online advertising metrics show you even more than just the money. **Metrics** are simply a way of measuring, or tracking, your campaign. Tracking the effectiveness and profitability of your online marketing campaigns allows you to move your marketing budget to the areas where it can give you the greatest return.

---

[19] http://imdb.com/title/tt0116695/

Determining Success

Assigning a value to success is key to determining the effectiveness of an advertising campaign. Even a sales lead has a value. If you close one out of every four sales leads, and the average sale is $1,000, then each lead is worth $250 gross—but if it costs you $100 in parts for each lead then it's only worth $150 in nett, so $150 is your acceptable cost per acquisition.

Cost per Conversion

Knowing how much each conversion costs is the key to determining the success of an online advertising campaign. For example, if we sell a $100 widget and make a 25% profit, we only have $25 to work with to stay profitable. If a conversion costs us $30, we're losing money.

Calculating Return on Investment

Return on investment, or ROI, is a financial measurement that shows the gains from an investment over time. Related to advertising, ROI is the percent return on your advertising dollars. You can use the following formula to calculate your return on investment.

((Revenue – Advertising Cost) ÷ Advertising Cost) × 100 = Your ROI (%)

When you're thinking about that revenue figure, you need to consider your profit margin. Out of every $100 widget, our gross profit is only $25. The rest goes to the product manufacturing cost, shipping, rent, salaries, or other expenses. Our total nett profit on $2,000 worth of widgets is only $500. So if we spent $1,000 on advertising, but only made $500, we've actually lost $500.

Calculating Profitability

While your return on investment is healthy when tracking sales with little or no costs associated with them, if you sell a product or service that has direct costs you need to know your **break-even point**. This is the revenue you need to make to sustain a profit while running an advertising campaign. If the campaign fails to generate enough revenue to reach the break-even point, the campaign will lose money. Here's how that works:

Advertising Cost ÷ Profit Margin = Break-even Point

Let's find out our break-even point for our previous widget example:

$1,000 ÷ 0.25 = $4,000

We can see that we have to generate more than $4,000 in revenue for every $1,000 spent on advertising for the campaign to be profitable.

Optimizing Based on Metrics

Having statistics only helps if you know what they mean, and how they apply to your bottom line. Optimizing your ads and conversion pages is one of the most valuable ways to spend your time. The improvements made will appear directly on your bottom line.

What is a Good Click-through Rate?

While a good click-through rate is subjective, depending on your niche, targeting, and other factors, if your click-through rate is over 4% it's considered favorable in almost any industry. A rate of 10% would be fantastic. If you're falling short of this, you'll need to optimize and test your ads.

Optimizing Ads

The first step to optimizing your ads is to test multiple ads. Google AdWords displays ads randomly at first, gradually learning which performs best. This is the default setting, and can be configured in Campaign Settings. Google will display the best performing ad most frequently while continuing to test ad alternatives and any new variation. Monitor your ads' performance regularly and pay attention to the following metrics:

1. click-through rate
2. conversion rate
3. total profit
4. ROI

The higher your click-through rate, the less you will pay for your ads. Google Ad-Words utilizes a Quality Score to determine ad rank. Your quality score is a secret formula that looks primarily at your click-through and conversion rates, as well as landing page quality, account history, relevancy, and other factors. In essence, the more effective your ads, the less you'll actually pay. So with increased conversion rates, you achieve lower costs as well!

Remove ads that perform poorly, replacing them with variations of ads that work better. Continue testing and improving on your ads regularly throughout your campaign. Test different offers and wording to see which are the most effective with your audience.

Advertising on Social Networks

Relatively new to the online advertising toolkit, social networking web sites such as Facebook, MySpace, and YouTube offer an alternative, and highly targeted, advertising solution. With hundreds of millions of users, many of which log in every single day, the big social networking web sites are advertising powerhouses.

Over two-thirds of the online US population is a member on one of the top three social networking web sites mentioned above. That's over half the total US population.

Social networking web sites are more than just growing, they're exploding! New visitors are joining by the masses, from all age demographics.

You've Never Seen Targeting Like This

Social networks know a lot of information about their members. Members readily give up their birthday, location, sexual orientation, relationship status, political and religious beliefs, and interests—all in the name of socializing with friends.

Ads on social networking web sites allow you to target according to virtually all of the information they collect about users—or at least the information users choose to make public.

If you sell a product targeted at 18- to 24-year-old guys who are college graduates, or 30-something mothers who are politically conservative, then advertising on social networks may be a really good fit for you. By advertising on social networking web sites, you're able to target criteria previously unavailable through other means, like search engine marketing.

Social networking sites may be unsuitable for some markets, though. If it's a bit tricky to segment your target market into the major demographics, it may be difficult to target. But if you're unable to find a way to target your potential customers using social networking web sites, you can still participate by creating a page or profile on the different social networking web sites. Let your customers and potential customers find you.

The Price is Right (Now)

Social networking web sites are growing rapidly, but advertising on them is still a relatively new marketplace. MySpace, Facebook, and YouTube are currently experimenting with different advertising and pricing models in order to determine which works best in this new medium. That means prices are cheap! Now is the time to start advertising on these web sites and take advantage of the low prices while they last.

Low Cost per Click

It's hard to advertise on search engines without paying 40 cents, a dollar, or even 10 dollars per click depending on the category and your rank, but you can advertise on social networking web sites for a mere 10 or 25 cents per click all day long on a large group of targeted users. Until more advertisers enter the market, these prices will stay low too, because they're market-driven and based on advertiser bids.

Look for Deals and Coupons

Advertising on social media is still so new that there are coupons and special promotions everywhere. Just try a search for "Facebook advertising coupons" and you'll see hundreds of dollars in free advertising just waiting for you to take advantage of.

Like an Old Friend

Advertising on social networking web sites should feel quite familiar to you if you've already set up a search engine marketing campaign. Apart from some minor differences, social network marketing is very similar to search engine marketing.

Banner and text advertisements are the most popular, as with search engine marketing. In some cases, small text ads can include a graphic as well as a headline and several lines of body text.

Normally, you can choose to pay by cost per mille or cost per click.

Tracking

Social networks have their own software for tracking impressions and clicks, just like Google AdWords or Yahoo Search Marketing. But they also work well with custom tracking links built for Google Analytics or other statistics software.

Facebook even claims to have real-time reporting of impressions and clicks, giving you minute-by-minute feedback on the effectiveness of your ad. There's no need to wait 24–48 hours to find out how your ads are performing!

Seize the Day!

Advertising on social networking web sites can be very effective if targeted, tested, and optimized. Now is definitely the time to try it out, because as more advertisers realize the benefits of advertising on social networks, those benefits will become less and less attractive as competition increases. If advertising on social networking web sites is a good fit with your target demographics, it's a great time to give it a go.

Using an Agency

Advertising agencies are sometimes portrayed in a negative light. Some people think that they charge insane hourly rates or require a retainer, that they're just a bunch of *creatives* sitting at tables *brainstorming*, or that they're still in the Stone Age and lack any experience of online advertising.

In truth, the right agency can help you plan, execute, and optimize your online marketing strategy, justifying their fees in the form of increased sales and profits.

Using an agency has its perks. Agencies can negotiate better advertising placements, gain your company PR when a new product or service launches, or help increase your online sales. Some of the benefits of an agency include:

Expertise and Experience	Even a small agency of 5–10 people has a wealth of experience that no one person could possess. When you hire an agency, you gain a team of experts who specialize in different segments of marketing.
Media Relationships	Agencies that offer public relations services often have strong media relationships, enabling them to more easily promote the message when there is a newsworthy story.
Outsourced Labor	When you hire an agency you're effectively hiring an entire marketing department without having to pay for salaries, taxes, and insurance. For the effective cost of one full-time jack-of-all-trades employee you can have a team of experts in several disciplines like design, development, and search engine marketing.

Should You Hire an Agency?

Choosing to hire an agency is a big decision that impacts your entire business as well as your wallet. To help you decide if hiring an agency is right for your business, here's a quick list of pointers:

Have a Reasonable Budget

Expertise costs money. Advertising costs money. Hiring a team of people with expertise in advertising costs a lot of money. While *reasonable* is a subjective word, you should be willing to allocate a substantial percentage of your operating budget to marketing if you intend to hire an agency. If your monthly marketing budget is $500 to $1,000, then hiring an agency might be beyond your means.

It's not uncommon for large companies to spend 5–10% of their annual revenues on the advertising and marketing budget. You have to pay for the expertise, planning, production and execution, as well as the actual advertising.

Invest the Time to Build a Successful Relationship

Hiring an advertising agency involves more than just providing some instructions and expecting them to come back in a month with an entire campaign, ready to rock'n'roll! Instead, the first few weeks—potentially months—involve a LOT of getting to know each other. In order to be successful your agency will have to become familiar with you, your product, and your target market—and that takes time.

Help Them Understand Your Business

An agency may have a lot of experience, but that doesn't mean they have a instant silver bullet for your business. Even with an experienced agency, it takes time to build a successful campaign.

For an agency to be able to help you sell your products or services, they need to know all about you. They need to know your trade secrets, your accomplishments, and even your problems. Knowing the big picture can help them determine how to best position you going forward. You can stop short of telling them how you pack and ship orders, but they need to understand you in order to determine the best marketing strategy for your business.

Through hiring an agency you may also discover that you know less about your customers or market than necessary to build a proper campaign; in this case your agency may actually assist you in doing research and learning more.

What to Look For When Choosing an Agency

Advertising agencies come in many shapes and sizes. Before hiring an agency you should consider the following:

Agency Size

If you're a small five-person company with less than seven-figure revenues, you'll be overlooked by many of the big ad agencies. Look for an agency that will give you personal attention. Be careful that the agency is large enough to handle the workload, given their current client base.

Experience

Online advertising experience is critical, and a prospective agency should have experience in your industry niche or marketing your type of business. They should be able to demonstrate through current and past clients that they can provide results for your business.

Testimonials and Case Studies

Client testimonials and case studies show what an agency can do, but you need to see actual results and speak with clients. Before hiring an agency make sure you first talk to one of their biggest clients. Ask them questions about the effectiveness of their marketing campaigns, the responsiveness of the agency staff, and so on.

Look for Personality

If you decide to look for an agency, shop around. Talk to several agencies and ultimately try and find one that fits with your company's personality. Make sure you like them, and they like you. You'll be working very closely with them for months or even years, so treat it as if you were hiring them all as employees. Would you want to come to work with them every day?

Smaller Budgets

Not ready to hire an advertising agency? If you need help, but lack the budget for a fully-fledged agency, consider hiring freelancers. Using a web site such as 99 Designs,[20] Guru.com,[21] oDesk,[22] or eLance[23]—or just by asking around—you can find freelancers that can help you with anything: from designing your web site to setting up your search engine marketing campaigns.

Freelancers' rates are often less than those of agencies, because they typically have fewer expenses and overheads. The downside to hiring freelancers is that it's unlikely any one person can perform the full range of online marketing services.

---

[20] http://99designs.com/

[21] http://guru.com/

[22] http://odesk.com/

[23] http://elance.com/

Advertising on Your Own Web Site

One of the most often forgotten advertising mediums is your own web site. Your current web site is an excellent place to advertise—your visitors are already looking at your site for information on your products or services, and they may be unaware of all you have to offer.

The Homepage

Homepages typically contain keyword-rich copy for the search engine's benefit, and then every department has their own contributions. There's news, recruitment, investor information, contact info … oh, and a link to your products and services in there also.

A significant portion of your homepage should be allocated to marketing. New products and specials should be prominently featured on the page for first-time visitors to see. It should change as often as possible. For ideas on the kinds of products or services you could market on your homepage, look to the campaigns and ad groups we created earlier in this chapter.

Up-sell

If you have a web application or subscription-based web site, you could offer upgrades. Personalize the web site to show upgrade opportunities and promotions in a way that's relevant to the user; that way they see offers that apply specifically to their current status.

If you restrict certain features or areas of your site to upgraded members, consider making those sections available to all members—but instead of showing all the content, show an example or teaser, and offer options for upgrading their accounts. A great example of this can be found at the *Wall Street Journal* online,[24] where each article has an excerpt available to general users, and a full article for subscribers.

You might also consider offering a second account for a spouse or child at a discounted price. There are lots of ways you can up-sell your customers; look for them!

---

[24] http://online.wsj.com/

Summary

The whole point of online marketing is to generate conversions in the form of leads, sales, or clicks, and advertising is one of the most visible ways to promote your brand. We've now covered how to target your online advertising, set up your campaign, and optimize your ads for the best results.

Tying It All Together

You've now learned about the many facets of online marketing—hopefully you're champing at the bit, ready to start campaigning!

Before you do jump out of the gates, we're going to take some time to plan your marketing strategy. Without some solid planning, you'll could end up running around in circles, unable to establish where the finish line is. In this chapter, we'll look at how to set realistic long- and short-terms goals for your online activity, and explore some methods of how to develop your own online marketing plan.

What have you learned so far?

Let's review what you've learned to this point.

Achieving the Best Possible Reach

You've learned how to write and distribute traditional press releases, that there are alternate ways to spread your news rather than just relying on the dailies, and that viral campaigns can gain you greater coverage than traditional press.

The centerpiece of your entire marketing plan should be a high-performing web site—and you now know the essential ingredients for building one. Usability and accessibility are critical elements of your design process, as well as page optimization tactics to maximize visitor conversions.

The Wonderful World of Search

You've gone beyond being just a user of search engines: you now have a greater appreciation of how they work. You're able to generate a campaign that delivers truckloads of new visitors to your web site, and you can do so in a way that targets only those people who are interested in your product.

The New Frontier of Social Media

Social media sites like Twitter and Facebook should now make more sense to you. Equipped with an understanding of how to effectively represent your business in social media circles, you're ready to start tapping into a broader market: by becoming part of a community, you'll form a strong, personal bond with your customers and prospects.

Engaging Email Marketing

With the wisdom that successful email marketing is about building relationships instead of pushing out sales messages, you're ready to expand on this rewarding, flexible, revenue-generating channel.

Affiliate Marketing

With an understanding of what affiliate marketing is, you realize that this model can help your business capture new audiences. There is an international army of high-performing sales agents willing to work hard at promoting your brand.

Online Advertising

You make every advertising dollar count. Aware of all the various types of online advertising, you can discern the difference between a program with potentially high returns and one that's little more than an expensive overhead.

Pick and Choose, or All of the Above?

You might have read over that list above and thought, "gee ... there's a lot to online marketing." You'd be right: when starting from scratch there's a lot of work involved, but it would be a mistake to just select one approach.

While some people will swear by a specific tactic, the key to ongoing success is spreading your revenue generation across multiple streams, just as it is with traditional marketing. That way, if one channel was to dry up, you're able to absorb the impact across other forms. Imagine what would happen if all of your sales came from search engine pay-per-click advertising, and increased demand for your target keywords drove prices to an unprofitable level? What if 90% of your traffic arrived via viral YouTube videos, and all of a sudden YouTube outlaws the use of links in videos?

By having a balanced marketing strategy, you'll be well-equipped to deal with the ups and downs of online marketing. With a balanced and stable core income, you can then try other initiatives without putting your business at risk. It's unrealistic to expect you'll have all your online activities ready in your first month, but as time passes, you should be aiming for multi-traffic, revenue-generating channels.

Creating Your Online Marketing Strategy

It's impossible to create a one-size-fits-all plan when it comes to online marketing. Here, we'll talk about how to create your own marketing plan that's tailored just for you.

The Idea

Chances are you've picked up this book because you have an idea for a web site, or you have a web site that's not generating the sort of income you think it should, or perhaps you're looking to launch your offline businesses on the Web. Regardless of your circumstances, it all starts with an idea—a chance at being better. With what you now know about how to successfully promote a business online, it's time to reflect a little, and decide if this really is a good idea. Do you have the time and commitment to do what it takes? Are you prepared for some hard work? If you can answer yes to both these questions, it's time to move to the next step.

Your Value Proposition

If you're already running a business, chances are you'll know what your value proposition is. For those that have yet to do so, it's time to establish your **value proposition:** what is the *benefit* your product or service provides to your customers?

Say, for example, you provide tandem skydiving for customers. The features of your skydiving experience might include safety and convenience, but as far as your customers are concerned, their reasons for buying will be all about how they *benefit*—in this case, the adrenalin rush of a lifetime. With every single campaign you run, remember that benefits create buyers.

Once you've nailed down your value proposition, you have the basis of your marketing message. When it's time to look for your customers, you'll have a strong message with which to promote your products or services.

Visualizing Your Journey

By now you've hopefully got a thousand ideas running through your mind but are struggling to make sense of it all. Whenever you find yourself in that position it's time to grab a notepad, write all your ideas down, then start to organize them into a sensible plan of attack. Write down everything that comes to mind, even if it seems silly or unfeasible. There are never any bad ideas, just poor planning and execution.

Finding Dependencies and Synergies

Once all your ideas are out in the open and in some sort of logical arrangement, it's time to start looking for **dependencies** and **synergies**. Dependencies are elements of your campaign that rely on other project factors for their success. Synergies, on the other hand, are outcomes that arise from the combined action of two or more factors. By looking for dependencies and synergies, you're able to see how each part of the plan can fit together, and gain a sense of which issues and problems could be tackled together.

For example, your plan of creating the world's most profitable affiliate program might first require a facelift of your web site, or your plan to send out your first email campaign would initially involve building a list of subscribers. You might also find that there are synergies between ideas; for example, by establishing a solid social networking presence, your followers may be more likely to blog about new announcements you make, thus providing solid links for your SEO endeavors. Another example could be that improvements in accessibility will have a flow-on effect of improving your customer reach and your site's search engine visibility.

Creating a Customer Contact Model

While creating your marketing plan, it's wise to add a customer contact model. This model helps you determine when and how a customer should receive a message from you. As well as marketing material, it should contain contact with your support team, interaction on social networking sites, and subscriptions to newsletters or RSS feeds. It allows you to understand what your perfect customer relationship looks like, as well as helping you to decide how frequently you should expose customers to marketing messages.

One easy way to understand your customer contact model is to draw it as a diagram. In Figure 9.1, I've sketched out a variety of ways a company could use to communicate with a customer.

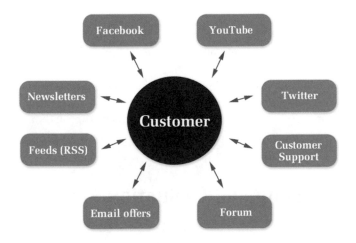

Figure 9.1. A customer communication model

Defining Customer Life Cycle Models

How well you convert new prospects into long-term customers can have a major impact on your revenue and profit. It's much easier to cross-sell or up-sell products to an established customer that has already developed a sense of trust and loyalty to your brand. Part of your marketing strategy should focus on how you build and maintain long-term customer relationships.

It's the same whether you're offering products or services. First and foremost you need to provide a quality, value-for-money offering, then be sure that you have exceptional customer support. You should also give your customers free reasons to come back to your site—such as a newsletter, complementary extras to a purchase, or special customer-only offers. Once the second purchase is made, the cycle simply continues. Figure 9.2 shows a fairly typical communications life cycle, beginning with the first purchase and using this two-pronged approach to lead the customer to a second purchase.

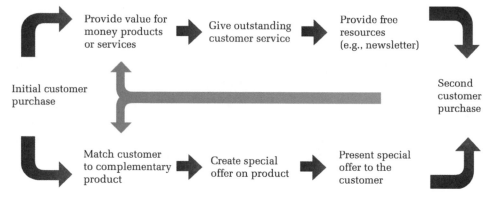

Figure 9.2. The two-pronged approach: excellent service and complementary products

As your business grows, you might choose to take this a step further with a dedicated customer loyalty program or rewards system. For now, a simple up-sell program is a great start.

Creating a Testing and Evaluation Plan

In just about every chapter of this book, focus has been placed on ongoing research and testing. The easiest way to ensure you're testing frequently enough is to include it as part of your marketing plan. Some of your marketing activities, such as advertising, email, and SEO, will require continual testing, as they change often. Others, such as usability and accessibility, require only occasional testing. You should detail the process that you'll use to test each method, as well as the frequency and measures of success.

Customer Research

You'll never hold all the answers to what makes an effective marketing plan, because customers can be a diverse lot, and you're just one person's opinion. A plan that may seem perfect for you could fall short in the eyes of your existing and potential customers. There's an obvious way to help understand your customers' needs better and that's to ask them to participate in a survey. Conducting surveys can be quite time-consuming, however, with customers often feeling like it's a lot of effort on their part for little reward.

Look to other avenues of communication—you'll find a wealth of information without having to ask. For example, analyzing your customer support enquiries can be a great source of insight, for both ends of the spectrum. If one person complains about a particular process or experience, chances are ten others feel the same way—but chose to remain silent. Keeping in touch with your customer support team is a great way to gaining some real-time customer intelligence.

Setting Goals

The core of any good plan is a set of goals. We all enjoy the success of hitting or exceeding a target, and such an achievement stimulates that ongoing desire to succeed, as well as helping to maintain high levels of motivation and determination. Goals also allow you to establish your priorities and maintain a focus, as everything you do in a campaign must in some way be linked back to your singular objective.

Establishing Goals That Are Measurable and Achievable

Goals need to be achievable. Otherwise they're not goals at all—they are dreams.

Goals must challenge you, but they also need to be realistic. You also must ensure that your goals are measurable. Otherwise, you'll never know if you've actually achieved them. For example, the goal "make $110,000 in revenues" can be concisely measured, compared to the more general "increase revenues."

Measurement must also include a deadline. Without having a firm set of goals that are achievable, measurable, and specific, you'll end up wandering through a marketing plan lacking direction.

Identifying Your Revenue Generators

If you have just one or a few products to sell, your online sources of income will be easy to identify. However, there may be some opportunities to supplement your income by adding new products that complement your existing business. Some of the common revenue-generation models you can try include:

- selling a new product which complements your offering
- offering advertising space to other sites
- participating in an affiliate program
- supplying an online service
- providing an offline service

For example, if you were selling an ebook about how to use a freelance job site like eLance[1] or Rent a Coder,[2] you could add to this by participating in the sites' affiliate programs, or delivering seminars on the topic to local businesses.

Once you've identified the areas you wish to branch out in, make a list of each income source, showing your current performance and your annual income targets, as shown in Table 9.1 below. I'd advise setting two targets: one that you realistically expect to meet, and one that you think you could reach if you stretch for your best possible outcome. You should always aspire to achieve your stretch targets, and treat your met targets as the bare minimum.

Table 9.1. Annual revenue growth targets

Channel	Current annual income	To meet	To stretch
Product Sales	$500,000	$600,000	$750,000
Advertising	$ nil	$20,000	$35,000
Affiliate program	$6,000	$8,000	$10,000

Identifying Your Key Performance Indicators

Ultimately revenue and profit will dictate your performance, but beneath your overriding targets will be a set of **key performance indicators** (KPIs)—measures

---

[1] http://elance.com/

[2] http://rentacoder.com/

that have a direct impact on your business performance. An example of key indicators could be:

- unique web site visitors
- number of sales
- revenue per visitor
- page views per visitor
- sample product downloads

Each of these statistics should be tracked at least monthly. By maintaining a vigil on these KPIs, you'll have early warning signs of performance drop-offs, as well as a starting point to identify potential sources of the problem. You should also set targets for your KPIs and revenue targets.

Milestones

Your revenue goals will most likely be based on annual targets, so it's important to set major and minor milestones for your program. This can include overall revenue targets, benchmarks for KPIs, and the achievement of specific tasks. Milestones can be easily visualized in your planning process—just draw yourself a timeline, like the one in Figure 9.3, and mark each goal.

Figure 9.3. An example of a timeline showing milestones

This process helps ensure your goals are achievable, and provides you with a marketing roadmap that integrates your revenue targets with your KPIs and specific channels. Using a timeline makes it easy to see what you need to do, and when.

Seasonal Variation

When setting monthly or quarterly targets for both revenue and KPIs, you need to factor in seasonal variation. For example, if you're selling Christmas decorations, it's likely to be quieter on early in the year, with growth increasing significantly leading into the festive season. If you're starting from scratch, you might be unable to accurately predict seasonal variations in your market; however, if it's obvious—as with the Christmas example—ensure you factor it into your plan.

The Stages of Marketing Planning

You should always have several marketing plans: for the short, medium, and long term. Multiple plans ensure that your business has a strategic vision for the future, plus details for the step-by-step processes you'll use to get there.

One plan may include details for your business growth over the next three years at an overall level, broken down by each year. Then, for some finer detail, create a 12-month plan that outlines everything you'll achieve in the calendar year. And finally, break the year down to a monthly level. This breaks down your plan into manageable, bite-sized chunks.

Writing a Detailed Campaign Plan

Okay: so you have your goals, some key performance indicators, and a roadmap; it's time to start dealing with the detail.

There are two ways to address a campaign plan. One way is to start with all your campaigns for the year, then detail each channel. The second method is to set targets for your channels and then detail the campaigns. Which method you choose (and you might do both) will depend on your perspective. If you're in charge of all marketing, then a campaign approach might suit; however, if you're responsible for a specific channel (say an affiliate program), then you may be wiser to start with your channel targets. Let's have a look at both.

A Campaign Approach

In this method we detail future campaigns, and then provide a drill-down view of each channel that will be utilized for each project. Here's a simple example of taking a campaign-by-campaign approach: we've grouped our tasks by campaign, and then listed how each channel fits in to the overall plan.

Campaign	Channel	Description
Product A launch	Launch of new product A	
	On-site	Create a dedicated landing page, update on-site advertising to promote product A
	Email	Sequence of three dedicated sales messages to existing customers
	Press	Distribute press release, identify and contact influential bloggers
	Social Media	Promote the new product on Twitter, create a Facebook group, and run a promotional giveaway
	Affiliates	Incentivize all affiliates with an extra $5 per sale
	Advertising	Implement Google AdWords campaign and CPI campaign through sitepoint.com
Birthday sale	Launch of new product B	
	On-site	Publish a blog post on the sale, update all on-site advertising
	Email Campaign	Sequence of three dedicated sales messages to existing customers
	Press Campaign	Distribute press release
	Social Media Campaign	Tweet the new campaign on Twitter, create a Facebook group, and provide a viral video of the "birthday party"

A Channel Approach

The alternative is to detail your plan by breaking it up into channels, then by campaign elements. This is ideal for ensuring that you have enough campaign activity to sustain a particular channel's revenue targets.

Channel	Campaign	Description
Affiliates	Launch of new product A	
	Product Launch A	Offer all affiliates an extra $5 per sale for the launch of Product A
	Affiliate Awards	Implement a suite of awards to reward high-performing affiliates
Social Networking	Launch of new product B	
	Twitaway	Complete a product giveaway to increase Twitter followers
	Facebook Fanclub	Create and attract followers to a Facebook group
	Forum Awards	Complete annual Forum-participation awards

For both methods, you'll need to ensure you're including targets for all campaigns (regardless of whether they're revenue-specific or not), as well as dates for implementation. Otherwise, rather than a real marketing plan, it will turn into a "someday, maybe" to-do list.

Your Marketing Plan

We've now gone through all the important elements that should be included in your marketing plan, from setting goals to specific campaign-level planning. This should be your security blanket when it comes to implementing your online marketing, and you should continually refer back to it if you find you need to regain focus. In the fast-paced world of online marketing, you can easily find yourself running a hundred miles an hour in all directions! With proper planning and a little discipline you can stay focused, spend your time on the important matters, and make the most of your online marketing activity.

Ready to Roll

So that's it—we reach the end. But where this book ends, your time begins. You're now ready to start your own online journey.

We hope you've enjoyed reading this book as much as we've enjoyed writing it. If you have any questions or feedback about the book, be sure to pop over to SitePoint and let us know.

Index

A

A/B testing, 47
ad groups, 139–140
advertising
    (*see also* online advertising)
    interruption, 79
    on social networks, 153–155
    on your own web site, 159
    search engine, 49
    spending, 130
    standard attributes, 133–135
    traditional, 129–131
advertising agencies, 155–158
advertising coupons, 154
advertising creative, 117
advertising on search engines, 138–150,
    162
    ad groups, 139–140
    campaigns, 139–140
    long tail, 141–142
    organizational structure, 139
    selecting keywords, 141–143
    where to advertise, 138–139
affiliate agreement, 123–124
affiliate marketing, 113–127, 162
    accuracy, 122–123
    affiliate agreement, 123–124
    and service providers, 121
    benefits, 114–115
    bonuses and incentives, 122
    choosing a system, 120–121
    cookie, 119
    cookie stuffing, 120
    dealing with bigger sites, 124
    definition, 114–121
    doubling up on leads, 115
    fraud, risk of, 116
    losing control of the marketing, 115
    minimum payout, 118
    programs, 114, 117–119
    prompt payment, 122–123
    recruiting affiliates, 124–127
    research your competitors, 126
    risks and pitfalls, 115–116
    technicalities, 119–120
    types of affiliate web sites, 116
    working with your affiliates for shared
        success, 125–126
    your commission model, 121–124
affiliate software, 120
affiliates
    recruiting, 124–127
    working with your affiliates for shared
        success, 125–126
agencies, advertising, 155–158
AllTop, 18, 83
Amazon, 114, 141
Anderson, Chris, 141
Andrews, James, 92
AOL chat rooms, 77
attracting visitors to your web site, 4

B

BackType, 30
banner ads, 129, 133
banner sizes, 146

banner sizes, online advertising and standard, 133

Barnes, J.A., 78

behavioural targeting, 136

black hat, search engine optimization (SEO), 53

blog aggregator, 83

bloggers, 9, 10, 14, 15, 20
how to pitch to, 20
influential, 20

blogging, 27, 90

blogs
and press releases, 17–21
commenting on influential, 19
influential, 18, 20
smaller copy bigger, 21

blog-specific search engines, 18

bookmarks and social media, 83

brand names
and keyword targeting, 58

brand representation, 33

break-even point, 151

Browsercam, 42

browsers, 41–42

budget, marketing, 131, 156, 158

budgets (search engine marketing), 147–149

Bulletin Board Systems, 77

C

campaign plan, writing a detailed
campaign approach, 170–171
channel approach, 172

campaigns, online marketing, 5, 131, 139–140, 149–150, 170–173
creating your campaign, 140

chat rooms, 77

click-through rate, 152

cloaking (SEO), 54

Comcast, 85

community development, 4

company policies, 27

cookie (affiliate marketing), 119

cookie stuffing, 120

cookies, 136

copyright and social media, 93

copywriters, 14

copywriting, 105

copywriting, SEO, 66

corporate information and homepage, 44

CPA – Cost per action, 135

CPC – Cost per click, 134, 148, 154

CPM – Cost per mille, 134

customer confidence, building, 46

customer contact model, 165

customer interaction, 5

customer life cycle models, 165–166

customer research, 167

customers, attracting and keeping, 33

D

Delicious, 83, 88

demographic targeting, 136

dependencies, 164

Digg, 88

Digg (social news web site), 83

direct sales messages (email marketing), 98

directories, 71

discrimination lawsuits, 38

display ads, 133

display ads, designing (online advertising), 145–147
ad copy, 146
ad formats, 147
design and graphics, 146–147
size of the ad, 146
tips for effective display ads, 147
distribution of press releases, 15–17

E

eBay, 114
ecommerce, 116
ecommerce web site, 35
eLance, 14, 158
email
and copywriting, 105
avoiding spam filters, 105–106
before you send, 107–108
best time to send, 109
building your list, 99–100
designing your, 102–108
different types of, 97–99
Excel spreadsheets, 100, 101
frequency and scheduling, 110–111
housekeeping, 98
HTML versus plain text, 106–107
managing your list, 101–102
message body, 104–105
message subject, 103–104
segmentation: targeting your emails, 109
sender's details, 102–103
sequencing, 110
technical side, 101–102
undeserved bad rap, 95–97
your landing page, 106

email marketing, 95–112, 162–167
and spam, 99
building your email list, 99–100
campaign, 95–97, 98, 101, 103, 107, 108–111
dangerous shortcuts, 100
direct sales messages, 98
educational communication, 97
measure, test, optimize and refine, 111
news and updates, 97–98
newsletters, 97, 99, 101, 104, 106
offline lead generation, 100
permission, 98–99
plannning your campaign, 108–111
try it for size, 101
types of communication, 97–98
undeserved bad rap, 95–97
emailing journalists directly, 15–16
emailing press releases, 15–16, 20
endorsements, 22
engage your audience, 4
entity, Web sites and evolving, 48
environmental marketing, 21

F

Facebook, 5, 29, 79, 87, 91, 154, 162
FedEx, 92
Firefox, 39, 42
Flash, 66, 134
Flash ads, 134
Flickr, 82, 88
focused terms, SEO strategy, 56
forums, 77
free newswires, 17

G

generic pages (web pages), 67
generic search terms, 55
geotargeting, 137
Godin, Seth, 132
Google, 29, 52, 53, 59, 138
Google AdWords, 138, 139, 141, 143, 145, 146, 152, 155
Google AdWords Keyword Tool, 142
Google AdWords Traffic Estimator, 142
Google Alerts, 29
Google Analytics, 155
Google Blog Search, 18
Google Chrome, 42
Google Keyword Tool, 57, 58, 59
Greteman Group, 27
guerilla marketing, 25
guerilla marketing campaign, 25
Guru.com, 158

H

hashtags, 29
hidden links (SEO), 54
homepage, 43–44, 48, 67
homepage and marketing, 159
homepage and press releases, 17
homepage design, 43
HTML, 66
HTML versus plain text (email), 106–107
hyperlinks, 11, 17, 64

I

iDevAffiliate, 120
industry data (online advertising), 138

Information

information collection, search engine, 51
information pages (web pages), 67
Interactive Advertising Bureau (IAB), 133
Internet Explorer, 42
interruption advertising, 79
interruption marketing, 79–80, 129
iPhone, 24

J

JavaScript, 66, 69, 134
JAWS, 39
Jennings, Jeanne S., 96
journalists
    and press releases, 27
    emailing directly, 15–16

K

key performance indicators (KPIs), 168
keyword targeting, 135–136
keywords
    advertising on search engines, 141–143
    generic, 55
    identifying your ideal, 57–58
    negative, 143
keywords, search engine optimization (SEO), 54–63
    add focused terms, 56–57
    advertiser demand, determining, 59
    common words, 57
    deciding which terms to target, 58
    identify generic, 55
    identifying current top performers, 59
    identifying your ideal, 57–58

link text, 60
localization, 58
modifiers, 56–57
phrases, 56
relevance, 60–61
return on investment, 62–63
singular and plural, 56
using brand names, 58
variations and misspellings, 56–57

L

landing page URL, 145
landing pages, 44–46, 48, 106
line marketing
    attracting visitors, 4
link text, 60
LinkedIn, 29, 87
links, 70–71
links, building incoming, 70
long tail (search engine marketing), 141–142

M

marketing
    (*see also* affiliate marketing; email
        marketing; online marketing)
    budget, 131, 156, 158
    environmental, 21
    guerilla, 25
    interruption, 79–80, 129
    on-site, 129
    permission, 132
    search engine, 49
    shock, 23
    undercover, 23
    word of mouth, 80

marketing campaign, guerilla, 25
marketing mix, 6
marketing offline, non-traditional, 21–23
marketing plan, 161, 163, 165, 166, 167,
    170, 172–173
marketing planning, stages, 170
marketing, non-traditional, 21–27
    online, 23–25
maximum cost per click, 148
media, 7–31
    (*see also* social media)
media kits, 14
media relationships, 156
meta elements, 65
metrics, online advertising, 150–153
Microsoft adCenter, 138
minimum payout (affiliate marketing
    program), 118
modifiers, SEO strategy, 56
monitor sizes, 42
MSN, 53, 138
multivariate testing, 47
MySpace, 5, 29, 87, 91, 154

N

99 Designs, 158
Netflix, 141
networking, social, 78
news release, 8
newsgroups, 77
Newsletters, 4
newsletters, 97, 99, 101, 104, 106
newswires
    free, 17
    online, 16
    paid PR, 16

non-traditional marketing, 21–27

non-traditional marketing offline, 21–23

non-traditional marketing online, 23–25

O

oDesk, 158

offline marketing, non-traditional, 21

online advertising, 129–160, 162

    advertising on search engines, 138–150

    advertising on your own web site, 159

    agencies, 155–158

    and ways to purchase, 134–135

    body of your ad, 144–145

    budget, 147–149

    choosing great targeted phrases, 142

    designing display ads, 145–147

    display ads, 133

    display URL, 145

    flash ads, 134

    highly targeted, 132

    homepage, 159

    how it is better?, 131–133

    interaction, 132–133

    launch your ads, 149–150

    long tail, 141–142

    measurability, 131

    metrics, 150–153

    optimizing ads, 152–153

    permission marketing, 132

    phrase matching, 142–143

    popunders, 134

    popups, 134

    pricing, 154

    rich media, 134

    social networks, 153–155

    standard advertising attributes, 133–135

    standard banner sizes, 133

    targeting for better results, 135–138

    text ads, 133, 143

    types of ads, 133–134

    up-sell, 159

    video ads, 134

    writing an effective ad, 143–145

    writing an effective headline, 144

online forums, 84

online marketing, 9

    and search engines, 162

    best possible reach, 161–162

    campaigns, 5, 131, 139–140, 149–150, 170–173

    changing the face of, 1–6

    creating a customer contact model, 165

    customer interaction, 5

    customer life cycle models, 165–166

    customer research, 167

    evaluation plan, creating and testing, 166

    expanding an existing business, 4

    global market, 5

    goal setting, 167–170

    goes beyond the Web geeks, 3

    instantaneous results, 5

    is about people, 2

    KPIs, 168–169

    milestones, 169

    non-traditional, 23–25

    opportunities, 6

    revenue generators, 168

    seasonal variation, 169–170

selling the owner, 26–27

social media, 162

starting a new business, 3

starting point, 3–4

steps, 4

strategy, creating your own, 163

technical, fast and complex, 2–3

transactions, 4

why is it so important, 2

online newswire, 14, 16, 17

online purchases, 46

on-site marketing, 129

Opera, 42

P

page layout, landing pages, 46

page title, 64

PageRank, 59

paid PR newswires, 16

past visitors, identifying, 136–137

permission and email marketing, 98–99

permission marketing, 132

photo sharing and social media, 82

photos, press release, 11

phrases, SEO strategy, 56

ping, 21

podcasts, 11, 83, 90

popunders, 134

popups, 129, 134

press coverage, modern monitoring of, 27–31

press release, 8–17

   21st Century, 9

   anatomy of a, 10–14

   and influential bloggers, 18–20

   content, 10–11, 12

   definition, 8

   distribution, 15–17

   distribution schemes, 14

   emailing, 15–16, 20

   length, 12

   making it stand out, 14–15

   official format, 13

   posting to your Web site, 17

   Someone wrote about me! what now?, 30–31

   what to include, 10

   writing a, 9

   writing services, 14

privacy and social media, 91

product pages (web pages), 67

product purchase, 4

profitability, determining, 151–152

public relations, 8–31, 156

   blogs, 17–21

   modern monitoring of press coverage, 27–31

   non-traditional marketing, 21–27

   press releases, 8–17

   responding to flattering comments, 30

   responding to negative comments, 19, 31

   Someone wrote about me! what now?, 30–31

purchasing (online advertising), 134–135

Q

Qik, 83

R

Really Simple Syndication (RSS), 16, 28

redirects (instructions), 69

return on investment, 62–63, 114, 151

revenue generators, 168

rich media ads, 134

roadmap, 170

RSS feeds, 4

S

Safari, 42

screen resolution, 42

search engine advertising, 49

search engine market, 53

search engine marketing, 49, 129, 135
 budget, 147–149

search engine optimization (SEO), 49–75
 and Web site design issues, 65–66
 black hat, 53
 content, 66–69
 copywriting, 66
 creating your own strategy, 54
 different hats, 53–54
 engaging the services of an expert, 74
 future of, 74
 keywords, 54–63
 measuring and tracking success, 73
 popularity, 69–72
 site design, 63–66
 spiders, 72–73
 white hat, 53

search engines, 162
 (*see also* advertising on search engines)
 cloaking, 54
 hidden links, 54
 information collection, 51
 measuring and tracking success, 73
 rank determination, 51–53

results pages, 50–51

role of, 50

site design, 63–66

understanding, 50–53

search engines results pages (SERPs), 50

seasonal variation, 169–170

selling the owner on online marketing,
 26–27

SEO Book Keyword Suggestion Tool, 142

sequencing (email), 110

SERP, 69

server performance, 69

service providers and affiliate marketing,
 121

shock marketing, 23

site design, search engine, 63–66
 heading elements, 63–64
 hyperlinks, 64
 issues and SEO, 65–66
 meta elements, 65
 page design elements, 63
 page title, 64
 paragraphs, 64

social bookmarking web sites, 83

social media, 78–93, 162
 and being human, 84–85
 and privacy, 91
 and spam, 89
 and transparency, 92
 blogging, 81–82
 bookmarks, 83
 definition, 78
 microblogging, 82
 mind-set, 84–85
 online forums, 84
 participation, 89–91

photo sharing, 82–83
podcasts, 83
policy, 92
problems and pitfalls, 91–93
social networking sites, 81
social news, 83
social profile, 91
starting off with, 85–91
trademarks and copywright, 93
types of, 81–84
video sharing, 82–83
word of mouth, 80
social media facilities, 11
social media monitoring services, 29–30
social networking, 78, 79, 80, 87
social networking web sites, 129, 153–155
social networks, advertising on, 153–155
social networks, tracking, 155
social news and social media, 83
social news web sites, 83
social profile, 91
social web sites, 77
spam, 89, 95, 99
spam filters, email, 105–106
spiders, 68–69, 72–73
StumbleUpon, 88
subscription-based web site, 159
summary pages (web pages), 67
SurveyMonkey, 137
synergies, 164

T

target keywords, 59
target.com, 38

targeting, online advertising, 135–138, 153–154
  behaviour targeting, 136
  demographic targeting, 136
  determining what to target, 137–138
  geotargeting, 137
  identifying past visitors, 136–137
  importance of targeting, 135
  keyword targeting, 135–136
TechCrunch, 18
Technorati, 18, 29, 83
television, 132–133
text ads, 133, 143
trackback, 21
tracking, online advertising, 155
Trackur, 29
trademarks and social media, 93
transactions, 4
transparency and social media, 92
Tumblr, 90
Twitter, 18, 29, 30, 87, 162
Twitter Search, 29
Twitterverse, 29

U

undercover marketing, 23
unique selling proposition, 144
unique visitors, 148
urban legend, 23
usability consultant, 37
usability testing, Web sites, 35–36
usability, Web site, 34–37
Ustream, 83

V

value proposition, 46, 164

video ads, 129, 134

video sharing and social media, 82–83

video, press release, 11

videos, 17, 24

visuals, landing page, 45

W

W3C's online validator, 39

Web browsers, 41–42

web development companies, 39

Web sites

  A/B testing, 47

  accessibility, 37–40

  accessibility, how to check, 39–40

  affiliate, types of, 116

  and evolving entity, 48

  attracting visitors, 4, 33

  browsers, 41–42

  customer confidence, 46

  customers, 33

  design, 63–66

  design issues and SEO, 65–66

  discrimination lawsuits, 38

  finding influential, 18

  homepage, 43–44

  landing pages, 44–46

  links, 70–72

  multivariate testing, 47

  performance, 40–41

  scalability, 41

  social, 77–93

  social bookmarking, 83

  social networking, 129, 153–155

  subscription-based, 159

  testing, 34–36, 42

  testing conversions, 46–48

usability, 34–37

  use cases, 35

white hat, search engine optimization (SEO), 53

word of mouth, 80

WordPress.com, 90

WordTracker, 60, 142

writing a detailed campaign plan, 170–173

writing an effective ad (online advertising), 143–145

writing an effective headline (online advertising), 144

Y

Yahoo, 53, 138

Yahoo Search Marketing, 155

YouTube, 82, 88, 154, 163

THE SEARCH ENGINE MARKETING KIT

BY DAN THIES & DAVE DAVIES

GROW YOUR SEARCH ENGINE TRAFFIC FROM SCRATCH

THE PRINCIPLES OF
PROJECT
MANAGEMENT

BY **MERI WILLIAMS**

THE PRINCIPLES OF
SUCCESSFUL
FREELANCING
BY **MILES BURKE**

THE
EMAIL
MARKETING
KIT

BY **JEANNE S. JENNINGS**

THE ULTIMATE EMAIL MARKETER'S BIBLE

SEXY WEB DESIGN

BY **ELLIOT JAY STOCKS**

CREATE YOUR OWN STUNNING WEB INTERFACES THAT JUST **WORK**

DELIVER
FIRST CLASS
WEB SITES

101 ESSENTIAL CHECKLISTS
BY SHIRLEY KAISER

ESSENTIAL CHECKLISTS FOR USABILITY, ACCESSIBILITY, AND MORE